Guidebook on Best Practices in Public Health

This work is published under the responsibility of the Secretary-General of the OECD. The opinions expressed and arguments employed herein do not necessarily reflect the official views of the Members of the OECD.

This document, as well as any data and map included herein, are without prejudice to the status of or sovereignty over any territory, to the delimitation of international frontiers and boundaries and to the name of any territory, city or area.

Please cite this publication as:
OECD (2022), *Guidebook on Best Practices in Public Health*, OECD Publishing, Paris, https://doi.org/10.1787/4f4913dd-en.

ISBN 978-92-64-96596-6 (print)
ISBN 978-92-64-84180-2 (pdf)

Photo credits: Cover © Cover design by Kathryn Frey using images from the following sources: Watch © Shutterstock.com/Natee Meepian; Father and daughter © Shutterstock.com/bbernard; Doctor © Shutterstock.com/Monkey business images; Cyclist © Shutterstock.com/Shift Drive.

Corrigenda to publications may be found on line at: www.oecd.org/about/publishing/corrigenda.htm.
© OECD 2022

The use of this work, whether digital or print, is governed by the Terms and Conditions to be found at https://www.oecd.org/termsandconditions.

Foreword

Changes in population structure, environments, lifestyle behaviours, and patterns of disease have led to growing public health challenges, such as increasing rates of non-communicable disease (NCDs), mental ill-health, air pollution as well as the rise of antimicrobial resistance. Many of these challenges were further exacerbated by COVID-19 and measures taken to curb the virus, in particular mental ill-health and physical inactivity.

This guidebook helps policy makers address these growing challenges by offering a tool to improve the rigour and reliability of selecting, implementing and evaluating public health interventions. It includes frameworks to identify best practice interventions that are transferable to a different region, and advice on the process for preparing and monitoring the implementation of an intervention once underway. It also covers the steps involved in designing and executing an evaluation study.

The guidebook is applicable to all types of public health interventions, such as those addressing key risk factors, managing NCDs, and the spread of infectious diseases. For example, health promotion actions delivered by primary care and other health care professionals, health literacy programs as well as policies to transform the environment in which people live. By facilitating the spread of best practice interventions, this guidebook contributes to efforts to reduce the health and economic burden caused by today's greatest public health challenges.

Acknowledgements

Jane Cheatley co-ordinated the production of the report and wrote Step 1. Martin Wenzl and Sabine Vuik were responsible for writing Steps 2 and 3, respectively. Overall guidance and strategic direction for this report was provided by Michele Cecchini.

The authors would like to thank participants to the Joint Action CHRODIS+ for close collaboration and inputs.

Preliminary versions of the guidebook were presented and discussed at the October 2020 OECD Expert Group on the Economics of Public Health (EGEPH), chaired by Amber Jessup, and at the June 2021 meeting of the OECD Health Committee, chaired by Hans Brug. The authors would like to thank all countries who provided feedback following these meetings, which provided essential input into the final report.

Special thanks goes to Artur Furtado from the European Commission who followed the development of the project since its conceptualisation and provided inputs throughout.

Francesca Colombo, Mark Pearson and Stefano Scarpetta provided valuable comments and suggestions at various stages of the project. Lucy Hulett provided essential support in the publication process, while Hannah Whybrow and Guillaume Haquin provided important administrative assistance.

This publication has been produced with the financial and substantive assistance of the European Union. The opinions expressed and arguments employed herein do not necessarily reflect the official views of the OECD member countries or the European Union.

Table of contents

Foreword	3
Acknowledgements	4
Executive summary	7
Introduction	10
Step 1. Select	**12**
1.1. Introduction to selecting an intervention	12
1.2. Step 1a: Identify best practice public health interventions	12
1.3. Step 1b: Assess transferability	24
1.4. Conclusion of Step 1	39
Step 2. Implement	**40**
2.1. Introduction to implementing an intervention	40
2.2. Step 2a: Preparing implementation	45
2.3. Step 2b: Implementing	56
2.4. Conclusion of Step 2	59
Step 3. Evaluate	**61**
3.1. Introduction to evaluating an intervention	61
3.2. Develop the evaluation study	63
3.3. Step 3a: Execute the evaluation study	74
3.4. Step 3b: Act on evaluation results	77
3.5. Conclusion of Step 3	79
Conclusion	80
References	81
Annex A. MCDA methodology	94
Annex B. Outcome indicators	96
Notes	103

FIGURES

Figure 1. Guidebook framework	11
Figure 1.1. Guidebook overview – Step 1: Select an intervention	12
Figure 2.1. Guidebook overview – Step 2: Implement an intervention	44
Figure 3.1. Guidebook overview – Step 3: Evaluate an intervention	62
Figure 3.2. Example programme logic for an intervention to reduce adolescent smoking	64
Figure 3.3. Example evaluation indicators across a logic model	66
Figure A A.1. Importance of criteria for assessing best practice interventions	95

TABLES

Table 1.1. OECD Best Practice Identification Framework criteria – the 5 E's	14
Table 1.2 Examples of priority population groups	17
Table 1.3. Study design typology	20
Table 1.4. Performance matrix template	22
Table 1.5. Weighted sums approach with minimum threshold score to define best practice	23
Table 1.6. Population context indicators	28
Table 1.7. Sector specific context indicators	30
Table 1.8. Political context indicators	34
Table 1.9. Economic context indicators	36
Table 2.1. Three interacting "systems" in implementation	42
Table 2.2. Key components of the implementation protocol	56
Table 3.1. Types of evaluation indicators	65
Table 3.2. OECD Well-being Framework – headline indicators	67
Table 3.3. Process for disseminating results	78
Table A B.1. Global indicators and aligning data sources	99

Follow OECD Publications on:

 http://twitter.com/OECD_Pubs

 http://www.facebook.com/OECDPublications

 http://www.linkedin.com/groups/OECD-Publications-4645871

 http://www.youtube.com/oecdilibrary

 http://www.oecd.org/oecddirect/

Executive summary

Countries face a range of public health challenges brought about by changes in lifestyle behaviours, environments, patterns of disease and population structure. These include increasing rates of non-communicable diseases and mental ill-health, air pollution and the rise of emerging infectious diseases such as antimicrobial resistance. Many of these trends worsened during the COVID-19 pandemic, in particular mental ill-health and physical inactivity as a result of measures designed to reduce contact between people. For example, prevalence of anxiety and depression more than doubled during the pandemic among OECD countries with available data.

This OECD guidebook assists policy makers in addressing the greatest public health challenges by outlining the process for selecting, implementing and evaluating public health interventions. Such interventions may include health promotion actions delivered by primary care and other health care professionals, health literacy programs as well as policies to transform the environment in which people live. Real-world experiences from member countries appear throughout the document to support theoretical frameworks that underpin the guidebook.

Step 1: Identify public health interventions considered best practice and appropriate for transfer

The first part of the guidebook assesses public health interventions against five best practice criteria:

- **Effectiveness**: Extent to which the objectives of the intervention were achieved;
- **Efficiency**: Extent to which inputs were used to achieve desired outcomes;
- **Equity**: Extent to which the intervention reduces inequalities in society;
- **Evidence-based**: The strength and validity of evidence used to develop or evaluate the intervention;
- **Extent of coverage**: Extent to which the intervention reached the target population.

For each criterion, the guidebook lists example indicators to assess performance, such as changes in quality-adjusted life years, life expectancy, and the cost-effectiveness or cost-benefit ratio.

Given the complexity of public health interventions, a best practice intervention in the original ("owner") implementation setting will not necessarily be a best practice in a different "target" setting. For this reason, the guidebook includes a framework outlining four contextual factors that affect the successful transfer of an intervention:

- **Population context**: covers population characteristics such as sociodemographic factors as well as broader cultural considerations;
- **Sector specific context**: covers governance/regulation, financing, workforce, capital and access arrangements in the sector the intervention operates;
- **Political context**: political will from key decision-makers to implement the intervention;

- **Economic context**: the affordability of the intervention in the target setting.

A comparison of the owner and target setting against these four contextual factors helps policy makers decide whether to transfer the intervention, and if so, what adaptions are needed.

For both the best practice and transferability frameworks, the guidebook outlines indicators – both publically available and those that require primary research – to assist policy makers select a public health intervention suited to their local context. Example indicators include population health needs; workforce volume, skills and culture; regulations and legislation; infrastructure; political priorities; levels of stakeholder support; and implementation and operating costs.

Step 2: Plan for and monitor implementation

Once an intervention has been identified as best practice and appropriate for transfer, the next step is to implement it in a new target setting. Laying out a formal implementation process is crucial given successful public health interventions rely on co-ordinated interactions between many people, tools and processes.

Step 2 of the guidebook provides a general framework for defining implementation in terms of "who does what, when". During the implementation phase, the guidebook sets out how to identify people who actively contribute to implementation and all other stakeholders; select measurable objectives and relevant implementation indicators; assess resource needs against existing capacity and readiness; build human and institutional capacity; identify additional contextual factors to plan integration with existing processes and workflows, and define the scope for further adaptation; and draft the implementation protocol.

After implementing an intervention, policy makers should provide ongoing monitoring and assistance to ensure its success. For example, by identifying additional resource needs as well as disseminating positive results to reinforce motivation and foster continued stakeholder support.

Step 3: Rigorously evaluate public health interventions

There are many reasons to support rigorous intervention evaluations. In particular, evaluating a newly implemented intervention is crucial to understand whether it is successful and should therefore be continued, or if the intervention needs to be amended or even cancelled. Despite the importance of evaluations, they are not always included in project plans, for example due to a lack of expertise, time and resources, or a "blind" belief in the intervention's success.

Developing an evaluation study should be undertaken once an intervention has been assessed as best practice and suitable for transfer. Designing the evaluation study at an early stage is necessary as it specifies the indicators and therefore the data needed to undertake an evaluation. To assist policy makers in this step, the types of indicators needed to measure effectiveness and efficiency are included, as well as tips on how to select those that are of high quality. Selected indicators were drawn from international databases, such as OECD Statistics and the World Health Organization's Global Health Observatory and are therefore universally recognised. Example indicators include changes in body-mass index, litres of alcohol consumed and the number of cigarettes smoked daily. Indicators also extend beyond health and include measures of well-being as outlined within OECD's Better Life Index such as life satisfaction. Finally, given it is not possible to rigorously evaluate all public health interventions, it is important at this stage to determine evaluation efforts based on intervention characteristics such as their size, significance and risk to population health.

Executing an evaluation study involves collecting primary and/or secondary sources of data to assess whether the intervention achieved its objectives. Data should be collected at the beginning and end of an intervention, and, if resources permit, a period after the intervention has concluded. Once collected, researchers must analyse the data, which includes choosing appropriate statistical methods to determine whether observed effects are due to the intervention or chance.

Results from the evaluation will guide follow-up action on whether to adopt, adapt or abandon the intervention. They should also be used to identify "lessons learnt", which can then be applied to future implementations.

Introduction

Changes in population structure, environments, lifestyle behaviours, and patterns of disease have led to growing public health challenges. These include, but are not limited to, increasing rates of non-communicable disease (NCD), poor mental health, air pollution as well as the rise of antimicrobial resistance (AMR). Such challenges are both a health and economic burden. For example, treating diseases related to overweight and obesity is expected to cost OECD countries, on average, USD 209 per person per year, which equates to 8.4% of total health spending (OECD, 2019[1]).

In response to these public health challenges, policy makers across the world are experimenting with different interventions that improve population health in a sustainable way. To assist the spread of interventions with a robust evidence-base, this guidebook outlines the steps policy makers can follow to select, implement and evaluate best practice public health interventions in their own country or region (Figure 1).

The three-step guide is based on the Plan-Do-Study-Act (PDSA) framework and can help reduce waste by encouraging policy makers not to "reinvent the wheel" (Ng and de Colombani, 2015[2]):

- **Step 1: Select (Plan)**
    - 1a: identify best practice interventions using a multi-criteria decision analysis framework
    - 1b: assess whether the best practice intervention can be transferred to a different context
- **Step 2: Implement (Do)**
    - 2a: prepare to implement the intervention
    - 2b: implement the intervention
- **Step 3: Evaluate (Study & Act)**
    - 3a: execute an evaluation by collecting and analysing data
    - 3b: act on evaluation results.

The contents of the guidebook are applicable to all public heath challenges. For this reason, it is important that **policy makers review and adapt material in the guidebook to suit their specific needs**. Further, although designed for policy makers, the guidebook is a useful reference for other stakeholders including those involved in planning, delivering and supporting the intervention.

Figure 1. Guidebook framework

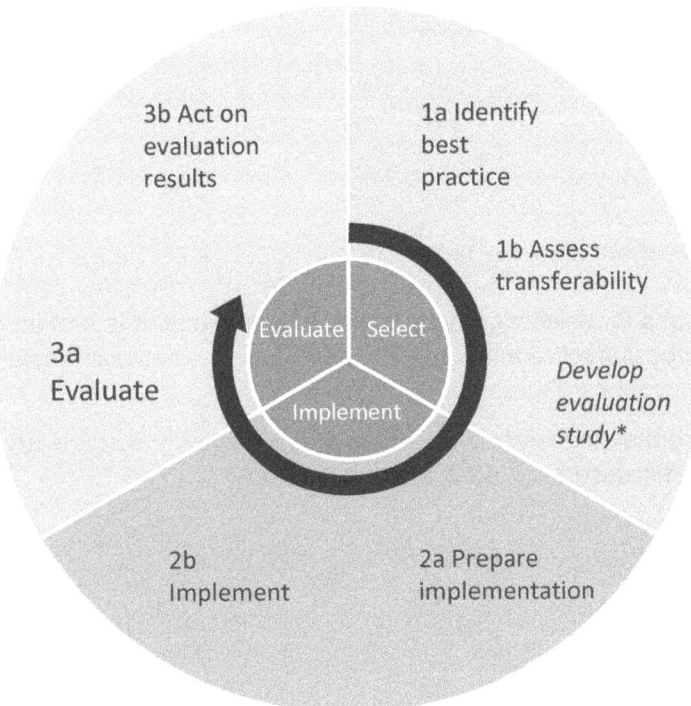

Note: *It is important to develop the evaluation study at the beginning of the cycle. Details on developing an evaluation are however discussed in detail in Step 3 (the "Evaluate" element of the cycle).

Step 1. Select

1.1. Introduction to selecting an intervention

Step 1 outlines the process for selecting best practice interventions. It is broken into two sequential sub-steps: Step 1a – identify best practice interventions; and Step 1b – assess transferability of a best practice intervention to a different context (Figure 1.1).

Identifying and assessing the transferability of a best practice intervention are key preliminary steps to the implementation process discussed in Step 2 of this guidebook.

Figure 1.1. Guidebook overview – Step 1: Select an intervention

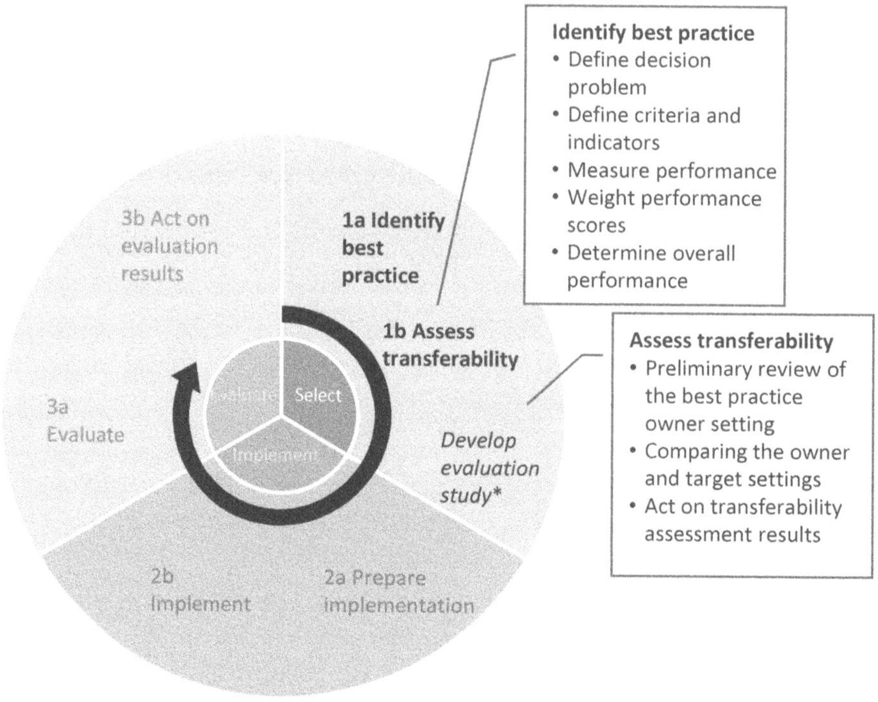

Identify best practice
- Define decision problem
- Define criteria and indicators
- Measure performance
- Weight performance scores
- Determine overall performance

Assess transferability
- Preliminary review of the best practice owner setting
- Comparing the owner and target settings
- Act on transferability assessment results

Note: *Details on developing an evaluation study are however discussed in detail in Step 3 ("Evaluate" element of the cycle).

1.2. Step 1a: Identify best practice public health interventions

To assist policy makers identify best practice interventions in public health, OECD has developed a high-level multi-criteria decision analysis (MCDA) framework – the OECD Best Practice Identification Framework (hereafter, the OECD Framework). An MCDA framework incorporates a range of criteria and aligning indicators relevant for evaluating a suite of alternative interventions. MCDA frameworks are a useful evidence-based decision-making tool given they provide a systematic approach to assessing the performance of interventions (Devlin and Sussex, 2011[3]; Thokala et al., 2016[4]).

The growing use of MCDAs in several sectors, including health, reflect the range of benefits this tool provides, as summarised in Box 1.1. MCDAs are particularly relevant for complex public health interventions as their impact cannot be measured by a single quantitative metric – i.e. a broader approach to assembling and analysing evidence is needed (Ng and de Colombani, 2015[2]; Rychetnik et al., 2002[5]).

Box 1.1. MCDA benefits

The benefits associated with using MCDAs to evaluate interventions and improve the decision-making process include:

- **Transparency**: criteria used to make decisions are explicit, as are the trade-offs between criteria (if weights are applied)
- **Objectivity**: by making the decision-making process explicit, decisions are made objectively and consistently
- **Complexity**: multiple, competing criteria, better reflect real-world decisions
- **Decision convergence**: engaging stakeholders with differing opinions to design the MCDA framework can facilitate decision convergence
- **Data collection**: MCDAs highlight criteria considered of most importance, and thus areas where data collection efforts should be enhanced

Source: Mühlbacher and Kaczynski (2016[6]), "Making Good Decisions in Healthcare with Multi-Criteria Decision Analysis: The Use, Current Research and Future Development of MCDA", https://doi.org/10.1007/s40258-015-0203-4; Phelps and Madhavan (2017[7]), "Using Multicriteria Approaches to Assess the Value of Health Care", https://doi.org/10.1016/j.jval.2016.11.011; Mandelblatt et al. (2017[8]), "Evaluating Frameworks That Provide Value Measures for Health Care Interventions", https://doi.org/10.1016/j.jval.2016.11.013.

The remainder of Step 1a outlines the process for identifying a best practice intervention using an MCDA approach. There are various methods for undertaking MCDAs, however, based on a review of the literature, the following high-level methodology was deemed most appropriate for public health interventions (Thokala et al., 2016[4]).

1.2.1. Defining the decision problem

The first step in undertaking an MCDA is to define the decision problem (Frazão et al., 2018[9]; Thokala et al., 2016[4]). This involves confirming at the outset:

- *What is the objective of undertaking the MCDA assessment?* For the purposes of this guidebook, the objective is to define public health interventions considered best practice. Policy makers may also wish to use the MCDA assessment to rank best practice public health interventions.
- *Which public health interventions are going to be assessed?* The types of public health interventions under consideration should be confirmed upfront given this will determine the final design of the decision framework (e.g. the indicators used).
- *What are the practical constraints in undertaking the assessment?* It is important to confirm the budget and timeline as these constraints will affect the design of the MCDA assessment (e.g. are there enough funds to collect new data? What is the timeframe for collecting participant data?)
- *Which stakeholders should be involved?* It is important to identify stakeholders whose input into the decision-making process is considered relevant and of high-value (e.g. defining indicators and

the relative importance of criteria). Engaging key stakeholders early on also enhances "buy in", which is critical to success (see Box 1.2 for information on identifying stakeholders). It is important to note that the list of stakeholders in Step 1 can differ from those involved in implementing and evaluating a best practice intervention. Further details on stakeholder engagement can be found in Step 2 (Implement), Section 2.2 of the guidebook.

> ### Box 1.2. Identifying stakeholders in Step 1a
>
> To identify stakeholders, start by "brainstorming" those whose value judgements are relevant to the decision problem (SELFIE 2020, 2017[10]). Types of stakeholders may include those responsible for implementing, participating or paying for the intervention. Further, given the technical nature of identifying best practice interventions, policy makers may also wish to include academics with experience undertaking similar analyses.
>
> Engaging the right stakeholders from the outset is important given it will lead to a higher quality assessment. Further, it can enhance the legitimacy of decisions made by policy makers thereby boosting public and professional acceptability.
>
> The final list of stakeholders should be diverse and, to the extent possible, focus on those who are underrepresented. Further, the list should avoid dominant stakeholder groups whose input may disproportionality shape decisions.
>
> Further details on engaging stakeholders can be found in Step 2 (Implement), Section 2.2.

1.2.2. Defining criteria and aligning indicators

Once the decision problem has been confirmed, the next step is to define the criteria to assess whether an intervention is a best practice. Drawing upon a review of the literature, expert feedback as well as existing public health MCDA frameworks, the OECD Framework applies five criteria – the five E's: **E**ffectiveness, **E**fficiency, **E**quity, **E**vidence-base and **E**xtent of coverage as described in Table 1.1.

To measure performance against each criterion, a range of indicators have been proposed. The list of indicators is intentionally broad in order to capture a wide range of public health interventions. Therefore, **policy makers are encouraged to only include indicators relevant to assessing the intervention(s) under examination**. This will simplify the process and avoid unnecessary data collection and analysis.

For further methodological details on how criteria and indicators were chosen, see Annex A.

Table 1.1. OECD Best Practice Identification Framework criteria – the 5 E's

Criteria	Definition
1. Effectiveness	Extent to which the objectives of the intervention were achieved
2. Efficiency	Extent to which inputs were used to achieve desired outcomes
3. Equity	Extent to which the intervention reduced inequalities in society
4. Evidence-base	The strength and validity of evidence used to develop or evaluate the intervention
5. Extent of coverage	Extent to which the intervention reached the target population

Note: Health Delegates to the OECD voted on the importance of criteria in 2019. Results from the vote can be found in Annex A.

Effectiveness

Definition

In the OECD Framework, effectiveness is defined as the **extent to which an intervention's desired outcomes[1] (objectives) were achieved in a real-world setting** (RE-AIM, 2020[11]; National Institute for Health and Care Excellence, 2020[12]; Productivity Commission, 2020[13]). Outcomes refer to the tangible impact associated with an intervention and can be classified as either intermediate or final. As an example, an intervention targeting obesity may measure fruit and vegetable consumption as an intermediate outcome and changes in body-mass index (BMI) as a final outcome (discussed further in Step 3 (Evaluate), Section 3.2.2) (Productivity Commission, 2020[13]; Mandel, Derx and Ilzkovitz, 2008[14]).

When assessing effectiveness, it is important to examine whether the intervention led to any unintended negative consequences as these may reduce or outweigh benefits (RE-AIM, 2020[11]). For example, a cycling to work scheme may increase physical activity levels, as intended, but also the number of injuries and emergency hospital visits.

Policy makers shouldn't necessarily disregard public health interventions with limited evidence given outcomes can take years to emerge. For this reason, policy makers are encouraged to consider interventions that have not yet been fully evaluated but which have a strong theoretical underpinning. Such interventions can be considered "promising" as they have the potential to become a best practice (Spencer et al., 2013[15]; Canadian Public Health Association, 2020[16]).

Finally, when assessing the effectiveness of different interventions, it is important to consider the timeframe in which outcomes are expected to be achieved. For example, school-based obesity interventions can look unfavourable against those targeting adults given diseases associated with obesity (e.g. cardiovascular diseases) don't usually appear until middle adulthood and therefore are unlikely to be captured within the evaluation time period. This is supported by previous OECD analyses which showed school-based obesity interventions are effective once a sufficient number of children exposed to the intervention are adults who are susceptible to developing chronic diseases (OECD, 2019[1]). Conversely, interventions to prevent complications for patients with diabetes may produce benefits in a shorter timeline since they target older, sicker patients, but are likely to cover a smaller share of the population and, in the long-run, may have a lower effectiveness.

Indicators

Indicators to measure effectiveness are split into universal health-related indicators and intervention specific indicators (Box 1.3). The former can be used to measure the relative effectiveness of interventions with different objectives by using a common outcome measure, such as quality-adjusted life years (QALYs). Although widely used, the validity and reliability of QALY measurements is often questioned – for example, alternate methods to measure QALYs can lead to markedly different results (e.g. standard gamble versus EQ-5D questionnaire), further, methods to collect data are not necessarily straightforward for patients leading to "nonsensical" results (Pettitt and Raza, 2016[17]). Instead, intervention specific indicators can be collected, which may be more appropriate. Intervention specific indicators can also be used as inputs to measure universal health-related indicators. For example, a change in BMI can be translated into a reduction in the relative risk of developing diabetes, which together with disability weights (a weight factor representing the severity of a disease) can be used to measure the change in disability-adjusted life years (DALYs). The OECD has developed a tool – the OECD SPHeP-NCDs (Strategic Public Health Planning for NCDs) microsimulation model – which can be used to carry out this type of analyses (For further details from OECD's SPHeP-NCDs model, see http://oecdpublichealthexplorer.org/ncd-doc/_2_1_Modelling_Principles.html).

> ### Box 1.3. Effectiveness indicators
>
> Example effectiveness indicators are listed below. These indicators have been chosen given they are internationally accepted and routinely collected in a standardised way. Users of this guidebook, however, should add/remove indicators as necessary (as is the case with indicators for all other best practice criteria).
>
> **Universal health-related effectiveness indicators**
>
> - Number of quality-adjusted life years (QALYs) gained (see Annex B, Box A B.2)
> - Number of disability-adjusted life years (DALYs) averted (see Annex B, Box A B.2)
> - Change in life expectancy
> - Change in healthy life expectancy
> - Change in perceived health status (% of participants in good or very good health)
>
> **Intervention specific indicators**
>
> A non-exhaustive list of indicators measuring effectiveness according to an intervention's objective(s) are in Annex B. This list covers interventions targeting public health issues such as key risks factors and chronic conditions.
>
> Source: OECD Health Statistics (2017[18]), "Health Status"; Sassi (2006[19]), "Calculating QALYs, comparing QALY and DALY calculations", https://doi.org/10.1093/heapol/czl018; European Commission (2021[20]), "Public Health Best Practice Portal", https://webgate.ec.europa.eu/dyna/bp-portal/.

Efficiency

Definition

Efficiency in the OECD Framework refers to **how well the mix of monetary and non-monetary inputs were used to achieve desired outcomes in a real-world setting** (European Commission, n.d.[21]) (Productivity Commission, 2020[13]).

Indicators

Efficiency indicators use effectiveness indicators and measure them in relation to inputs used. Therefore, efficiency indicators have also been broken into those that are universal or intervention specific (see Box 1.4). The economic evaluation methods used to measure efficiency indicators are discussed in Step 3 (Evaluate), Box 3.7.

Data for economic evaluations is often difficult to obtain for public health interventions (CHRODIS, 2015[22]). Therefore, interventions with limited efficiency data shouldn't automatically be disregarded (e.g. they could instead be classified as a promising intervention).

> **Box 1.4. Efficiency indicators**
>
> Efficiency indicators measure how well resources were used to achieve desired outcomes. Universal indicators can be used when the outcome is expressed in a common unit (e.g. QALY), and are useful when comparing different types of interventions. Conversely, intervention efficiency indicators compare resources to intervention specific outcomes.
>
> **Universal health-related efficiency indicators**
>
> - Incremental cost-effectiveness ratio – i.e. cost per QALY gained or cost per DALY averted
> - Cost-benefit ratio (where costs and benefits are both expressed in monetary terms)
>
> **Intervention specific efficiency indicators**
>
> - Incremental cost-effectiveness ratio for specific health outcome – e.g. cost per 1-point reduction in BMI / 1cm reduction in waist circumference

Equity

Definition

Equity measures **whether an intervention reduces inequalities in society** and is a basic requirement of any public health intervention (Ng and de Colombani, 2015[2]; European Commission Directorate General for Health and Food Safety, 2017[23]).

Measuring the impact of an intervention on inequality involves an assessment of two key concepts – access and outcomes – across different population groups (Lehne et al., 2019[24]). That is, did access to, and outcomes from, the intervention differ across population groups (NEJM, 2020[25]). Population groups of interest are those that are underserved and therefore at greater risk of adverse health outcomes – i.e. priority population groups (see Table 1.2 for examples) (Public Health Ontario, 2015[26]). In addition to priority population groups, it is important to analyse results by age and gender.

Table 1.2 Examples of priority population groups

Demographic and socio-economic factors	Priority population group
Geography	Individuals residing in **regional/remote areas** typically experience greater inequities in accessing health care
Ethnicity and indigenous status	**Ethnic minority groups** and **certain indigenous populations** often experience worse health outcomes
Education status	Those with a **lower level of education** typically experience worse health outcomes
Employment status and income	Those who are **unemployed** and/or on a **lower income** typically experience worse health outcomes

Source: Walker, Strom Williams and Egede (2016[27]), "Influence of Race, Ethnicity and Social Determinants of Health on Diabetes Outcomes", https://doi.org/10.1016/j.amjms.2016.01.008; Snijder (2017[28]), "Cohort profile: Healthy Life in an Urban Setting (HELIUS) study in Amsterdam, the Netherlands", http://dx.doi.org/10.1136/bmjopen-2017-017873; NEJM (2020[25]), "Social Determinants of Health (SDOH)", https://catalyst.nejm.org/doi/full/10.1056/CAT.17.0312; Phillips (2005[29]), "Defining and measuring gender: A social determinant of health whose time has come", https://doi.org/10.1186/1475-9276-4-11.

Interventions that reduce heath inequalities may not necessarily be the most efficient, that is, there may be an equity-efficiency trade-off (Cookson, Drummond and Weatherly, 2009[30]). For example, it may be more efficient to implement a public health campaign in a highly populated area to maximise participation, however, this would be at the expense of those living in regional/rural areas. Consequently, the gap in access between the two groups would widen. Policy makers are encouraged to take this trade-off into account when making decisions to ensure an equitable distribution of resources.

Indicators

Indicators to measure an intervention's impact on reducing societal inequalities are outlined in Box 1.5.

Box 1.5. Equity indicators

Access

- Differences in participation rates across population groups (see Box 1.7)
- Differences in dropout rates across population groups (see Box 1.7)

Outcomes

- Differences in effectiveness indicators across population groups (see Box 1.3)

Intervention design

- The needs of priority population groups were considered when designing the intervention
- A process was used to identify priority populations who would benefit from the intervention

Source: European Commission (2021[20]), "Public Health Best Practice Portal", https://webgate.ec.europa.eu/dyna/bp-portal/; Cookson et al. (2016[31]), "Healthy Equity Indicators for the English NHS: a longitudinal whole-population study at the small-area level", https://doi.org/10.3310/hsdr04260; CHRODIS, (2015[22])"Task 1: selecting JA-CHRODIS criteria to assess good practice in interventions related to chronic conditions", http://chrodis.eu/wp-content/uploads/2016/03/Delphi-2_MULTIMORBID.pdf.

Evidence-base

Definition

The evidence-base criterion reflects **the quality of evidence to develop or evaluate an intervention**. Assessment of the former (i.e. to develop an intervention) is important for identifying promising interventions for which evidence is still limited. Conversely, assessment of the latter (i.e. to evaluate an intervention) is important for checking the robustness of outcome evaluations for established interventions. It is a cross-cutting criterion given it relates to the quality of evidence on outcomes which are used in effectiveness, efficiency and selected equity indicators.

Guides to assess the level of evidence in terms of outcomes classify types of evidence by their potential to eliminate bias and establish causality. Therefore, they are an important tool for assessing the strength and validity of outcome evaluation results.

Randomised controlled trials (RCTs), which primarily focus on individuals, are considered the "gold standard" (see Box 3.5 in Step 3 (Evaluate) for further details on RCTs) (Rychetnik et al., 2002[5]). RCTs, however, are often not applicable to public health interventions. For example, it may not be possible to create a control group if it is unethical or impossible to exclude people from accessing an intervention. RCTs can also be expensive to carry out and are associated with their own limitations (e.g. selection bias of those who receive treatment) (Deaton and Cartwright, 2018[32]). For these reasons, it is important to consider other forms of data collection and analyses better suited for public health such as observational studies (Barnish and Turner, 2017[33]).

High-quality evidence is more readily available for easy-to-reach populations such as those living in cities with access to the internet and mobile phones (Rychetnik et al., 2002[5]). Conversely, data from hard-to-reach or "hidden" populations (e.g. homeless, migrants, lower socio-economic status) (Bonevski et al., 2014[34]), can be difficult to obtain thereby downgrading the quality of evidence for interventions targeting these populations (Rychetnik et al., 2002[5]). For this reason, flexibility when assessing the evidence-base of an intervention is needed to ensure an equitable distribution of public health resources (Rychetnik et al., 2002[5]).

Indicators

Evidence-based indicators have been classified into a three-tiered hierarchy (Box 1.6). The evidence-base hierarchy is designed to provide policy makers with a rapid appraisal of a study's internal validity (i.e. the extent to which outcomes achieved can be attributed to the intervention). For each level of evidence, systematic reviews or meta-analyses combining multiple studies are preferable to a single intervention study.

Studies using the same design are not necessarily of the same quality. Therefore, a second assessment of a study's internal validity is recommended (e.g. by examining whether the research design exhibits any signs of bias such as selection, performance, detection, attrition and/or reporting bias (Berkman et al., 2014[35])). The *Quality Assessment Tool for Quantitative Studies* developed as part of the Effective Public Health Practice Project provides a standardised method for assessing the quality of public health intervention studies (see https://merst.ca/wp-content/uploads/2018/02/quality-assessment-tool_2010.pdf). The tool is designed as a questionnaire (intended to take between 30-60 minutes to complete) and consists of eight components to assess study quality. Results from the questionnaire allow users to rate the quality of evidence as either strong, moderate or weak (Effective Public Health Pratice Project, 1998[36]). Another option is to use the GRADE (Grading of Recommendations, Assessment, Development and Evaluations) approach, which outlines several domains that rate up or down the certainty of study results (Guyatt et al., 2011[37]). GRADE is one of the most widely used approaches to evaluate the quality of evidence, but its use on public health studies has been more limited and its applicability in this field is still debated (for example, see (Irving et al., 2016[38]; Rehfuess, Bruce and Pruss-Ustun, 2011[39])).

> **Box 1.6. Evidence-base indicators**
>
> Evidence-based indicators have been classified into a three-tiered hierarchy. The hierarchy is high-level, therefore, it is important to examine the quality of the study design in further detail. For example, a well-designed cohort study may be of higher quality than a poorly designed RCT.
>
> **Study design hierarchy** (see Table 1.3 for further explanation)
>
> *High-quality evidence*
> - Randomised controlled trials (RCTs)
>
> *Medium-quality evidence*
> - Non-randomised control trial
> - Pre-post studies
> - Cohort studies (prospective or retrospective)
> - Case-control studies
> - Cross-sectional studies
> - Ecological studies

Low-quality evidence
- Patient experiences
- Case studies
- Expert opinion
- Mechanism-based reasoning

Table 1.3. Study design typology

Quality level	Study design	Description
High	RCTs	Subjects in a population are randomly allocated into one of two groups: study group (receive the intervention) or control group (do not receive the intervention)
Medium	Non-randomised control trial	Compares the outcomes of the participants of the intervention to another group of people who did not participate in the trial
	Pre-post study	Compares the outcomes in the study population before and after the intervention – ascribing a change in the outcome to the intervention
	Prospective cohort studies	Follow a group of individuals over time who differ by a certain characteristic to determine whether that characteristic influences certain outcomes
	Retrospective cohort studies	As above but using previously collected data
	Case-control studies	Analysis of two groups, one that exhibits the outcome of the interest, the other not. Retrospectively researchers determine which individuals were exposed to the intervention/treatment
	Cross-sectional studies	Analyses of data collected at a specific point in time across a sample population
	Ecological studies	Observational study based on data collected at the population or group level. They are typically used to measure disease prevalence and incidence.
Low	Participant experience, case-study, and expert opinion data	Considers qualitative data collected directly from participants, stakeholders and/or experts to understand the impact of an intervention (e.g. through interviews, surveys)
	Mechanism-based reasoning	Involves an inference from mechanisms to claims that an intervention produces a patient-relevant outcome

Source: Mann (2003[40]), "Observational research methods. Research design II: Cohort, cross sectional, and case-control studies", http://dx.doi.org/10.1136/emj.20.1.54; Oxford University (2016[41]), "OCEBM Levels of Evidence", https://www.cebm.net/2016/05/ocebm-levels-of-evidence/; U.S. Preventive Services Taskforce (2017[42]), "Section 4. Evidence Review Development", https://www.uspreventiveservicestaskforce.org/uspstf/section-4-evidence-review-development; Rychetnik et al. (2002[5]), "Criteria for evaluating evidence on public health interventions", http://dx.doi.org/10.1136/jech.56.2.119.

Extent of coverage

Definition

"Extent of coverage" refers to the **extent to which the intervention reached the target population** (RE-AIM, 2020[11]) Assessing this criterion is important for understanding the intervention's success in recruiting eligible participants, that is, those who stand to benefit most (Spencer et al., 2013[15]; RE-AIM, 2020[11]).

Indicators

Extent of coverage indicators are broken into two groups: individual and organisation level indicators (see Box 1.7). The former closely aligns with the "Reach" indicator in the RE-AIM framework, which measures the proportion of the eligible population who accessed the intervention (RE-AIM, 2020[11]). Organisation-level indicators refer to participation of providers (e.g. primary care practices, schools, health clinics) responsible for delivering the intervention (CDC, 2011[43]).

Individual and organisation indicators are intertwined given a higher number of participating organisations will lead to a higher individual participation rate. Nevertheless, collecting organisational-level data is important as it may provide insights into why some population groups access an intervention and others do not.

> **Box 1.7. Extent of coverage indicators**
>
> **Individual level indicators**
>
> - Proportion of the eligible population who accessed the intervention (individual participation rate)
> - Proportion of individuals enrolled in the intervention who subsequently dropped out (individual dropout rate)
>
> **Organisation level indicators**
>
> - Proportion of providers responsible for delivering the intervention who participate (provider participation rate)
> - Proportion of providers enrolled in the intervention who subsequently dropped out (provider dropout rate)
>
> Source: RE-AIM (2020[11]), "Reach", http://www.re-aim.org/about/what-is-re-aim/reach/; CDC (2011[43]), "Program Evaluation Tip Sheet: Reach and impact", https://www.cdc.gov/dhdsp/programs/spha/docs/reach_impact_tip_sheet.pdf.

1.2.3. Measuring performance

Once criteria and indicators are defined, the next step is to collect data to measure the performance of each intervention. Indicators proposed as part of OECD's Framework are universally recognised, further, in regards to effectiveness indicators, they have been drawn from publically available databases (see Annex B for a list of these databases). This has two major benefits: 1) it reduces the burden associated with collecting data; and 2) it makes it easier for policy makers to compare the performance of different interventions. Where it has been determined that a specific indicator is of high importance but for which there is no available data, policy makers can rely on feedback from stakeholders/experts or the literature to measure performance.[2]

A "performance matrix" can be used to record results. An example performance matrix template focused on obesity prevention interventions is provided in Table 1.4. For a real-world example, see Marsh et al. (2013[44]) – Table 3 – who used an MCDA to assess a range of preventive health interventions (Marsh et al., 2013[44]).

To enhance the interpretability of results, policy makers may wish to convert "natural performance measures" in the performance matrix to quantitative scores. That is, convert measurements into units which are common across all criteria (such as from 0-100). The quantitative scale should reflect the best and worst score that is realistically possible (SELFIE 2020, 2017[10]). **This type of analysis is only appropriate when comparing interventions measuring the same indicators.**

Further details on the varied ways of converting performance measurements into quantitative scores, see the *OECD's Handbook On Constructing Composite Indicators: methodology and user guide* (OECD and European Commission, 2008[45]).

Table 1.4. Performance matrix template

Intervention	% change in BMI (effectiveness)	Cost per 1-point reduction in BMI (efficiency)	Distribution of benefits ratio* (equity)	Quality of evidence (evidence-base)	Participation rate (extent of coverage)
School-based intervention					
Prescription of physical activity					
Food labelling					
Nutrition mHealth app					

Note: This is an example performance matrix only. It is simplified and therefore should not be used a final framework for assessing obesity prevention interventions. *Based on (Marsh et al., 2013[44]), the distribution of benefit ratio represents the ratio of the proportion of the most disadvantaged 20% of the population eligible for the intervention to the proportion of the population as a whole eligible for the intervention.

1.2.4. Weighting performance scores

The importance of criteria for assessing best practice will likely differ. Therefore, it may be appropriate to assign weights to each criteria (for example, using feedback from stakeholders).

There exist multiple methods to elicit weights, of most relevance to public health are discrete choice experiments and swing weighting given they force individuals to make trade-offs between criteria:

- **Discrete choice experiments (DCE):** in DCE, individuals are asked to compare various interventions which systematically differ on performance criteria. Individuals are then prompted to specify between two or more interventions, which they prefer. By doing so, individuals are forced to make trade-offs which reveal criteria they deem most important.
- **Swing weighting:** swing weighting begins with all interventions scoring the lowest possible score (worst-case scenario). From here, individuals are asked which criteria, if improved, would lead to the greatest overall gain. This process is then repeated for all remaining criteria to create a ranked scale, which are then transformed into weights.

Although considered methodologically more robust, the above two methods are relatively resource intensive. Therefore, policy makers may wish to consider straightforward weighting methods such as:

- **Visual analogue scale (VAS):** VAS present individuals with a visual scale ranging from 0 (not important) to 100 (very important), for example, for each criteria. Individuals are then asked to pinpoint the importance of the criteria on the provided scale. If weights do not add up to 100, they must be re-scaled. One possible downside of using this method is the potential for individuals to rank the importance of each criteria highly.
- **Point allocation:** individuals are provided with the list of all criteria and asked to divide 100 points between them, with higher points reflecting greater importance.

For further details on each of the aforementioned weighting methods, and more, see the following European Commission (EC) report (SELFIE 2020, 2017[10]).

Based on feedback from delegates within OECD's Expert Group for the Economics of Public Health and previous work undertaken by the EC, **effectiveness, efficiency and equity are considered high priority indicators**. Specifically, each of these are considered core criteria within EC's tool for selecting best practices, further, between 72-94% of OECD delegates voted they were either "important" or "necessary" (see Annex A for full results).

1.2.5. Determining overall performance

Two possible methods for determining best practice interventions are proposed in this section: 1) setting a minimum overall performance score threshold or 2) setting a minimum performance score threshold for each criterion.

Despite which approach is used, it is important that the methodology to determine best practice interventions is transparent. This involves reporting and justifying criteria and indicators used to measure performance; weights applied to criteria; and the process for developing a minimum threshold score.

Minimum overall performance score threshold

This method sums the weighted quantitative scores for each criteria to obtain an overall score (often referred to as a "global score"). An example template using the weighted sums approach is provided in Table 1.5 (this is an example only; it does *not* reflect weights or scores previously defined in another study).

Next, based on feedback from policy makers and stakeholders, a minimum threshold overall score is defined. Interventions with an overall score at or above the threshold are considered best practice and not best practice, if below. This approach is currently used by the EC to identify good and best practice interventions (see (European Commission, n.d.[46])).

As a robustness check, policy makers may wish to undertake deterministic sensitivity analysis. This type of analysis involves changing parameters within the OECD Framework and assessing how this affects results. For example, how do results differ based on a change in weights allocated to criteria? (Marsh et al., 2013[44]).

Table 1.5. Weighted sums approach with minimum threshold score to define best practice

Intervention	% change in BMI	Cost per 1-point reduction in BMI	Distribution of benefits ratio	Quality of evidence to evaluate intervention	Participation rate	**Overall score**
Weights	20% (=0.20)	30% (=0.30)	10% (=0.10)	30% (=0.30)	10% (=0.10)	**100% (=1)**
School-based intervention	80	40	50	90	80	**69**
Nutrition mHealth app	30	80	60	10	90	**48**
Best practice minimum threshold score = 40						
Prescription of physical activity	70	30	40	20	20	**35**
Food labelling	40	20	70	20	40	**31**

Note: This is an example performance matrix only. It does **not** reflect weights or scores estimated during a systematic MCDA assessment. For example, school-based intervention: Overall score 69 = 80*0.2 + 40*03 + 50*0.1 + 90*0.3 + 80*0.1.

Minimum performance score threshold for each criterion

Using an overall performance score to determine best practice interventions can lead to misleading results as it is assumed that a low score for one criterion can be offset by a high score in another. For example, despite the use of weights, an intervention with the following characteristics could be wrongly assessed as best practice:

- Targets a priority population group to advance health equity
- Was evaluated using high quality evidence

- Achieves a high participation rate and experiences low drop out
- Does *not* lead to a significant improvement in outcomes.

To overcome this issue, minimum threshold scores for each criteria can be developed. Minimum threshold scores can be based on standardised quantitative score or natural performance scores. For example, for a public health intervention to be classified as "best" by the EC it is must meet a minimum score on "exclusion criteria" (e.g. whether the intervention is a public health political priority, and the quality of the evidence base) (European Commission, n.d.[46]).

1.2.6. Next steps

The OECD Framework can assist policy makers identify public health interventions that are best practice based on performance within a specific setting. An intervention classified as best practice should not immediately be considered appropriate for implementation in another setting given the impact of external factors. For this reason, prior to implementation (Step 2), it is important to determine whether the intervention is transferable.

1.3. Step 1b: Assess transferability

Public health interventions are complex given they involve several interacting components and multiple stakeholders in areas such as health, education, community and environment; often target heterogenous populations; and have outcomes influenced by various direct and indirect factors (Craig et al., 2008[47]; Norris et al., 2019[48]). Therefore, policy makers cannot assume positive outcomes achieved in one setting can automatically be transferred to a different setting (Schloemer and Schröder-Bäck, 2018[49]).

Step 1b assesses whether the identified best practice intervention is "transferable". For the purpose of this guidebook, an intervention is defined as transferable if desired outcomes achieved in a given setting can be achieved in another well-defined setting (Trompette et al., 2014[50]; Burchett, Umoquit and Dobrow, 2011[51]). The assessment is broken into two components. First, a preliminary review of the best practice intervention in the setting where it has been proven successful (i.e. the best practice "owner setting"). And, second, comparing the owner setting with the "target setting", that is, where policy makers intend to transfer the best practice (Wang, Moss and Hiller, 2006[52]; Schloemer and Schröder-Bäck, 2018[49]).

The process for assessing transferability addresses many of the same factors used to assess sustainability as summarised in Box 1.8.

> **Box 1.8. Sustainability of public health interventions**
>
> There is no agreed term to define "sustainability", in general, however, it refers to the ability to maintain an intervention and its aligning benefits in the long term. Sustainability is often viewed through the lens of funding (i.e. affordability), yet it is far more complex than this (Bodkin and Hakimi, 2020[53]).
>
> Several frameworks to assess sustainability are available, however, no framework dominates, further, they are not validated. Nevertheless, there are factors common to several frameworks, many of which are covered in Step 1b – assess transferability – such as (Bodkin and Hakimi, 2020[53]):
>
> - *Political support*: assessing the political environment that determines which interventions are prioritised.
> - *Affordability*: whether there is a stable funding environment.
> - *Organisational capacity*: whether there are appropriate resources to deliver intervention activities (e.g. qualified staff).
> - *"Champions"*: whether there is a champion(s) to advocate for the intervention.
> - *Fit/alignment*: whether the intervention fits with existing interventions and aligns with community needs.
> - *Adaption*: whether the intervention is adapted to suit the needs of the target setting.
>
> Sustainability is also considered in Step 2 – Implement – and Step 3 – Evaluate – of the guidebook. That is, an intervention is more likely to be sustainable if it is implemented following a thorough preparation phase involving key stakeholders, and evaluated in order to demonstrate its value.

This guidebook outlines four contextual factors affecting the successful transfer of an intervention. These four contextual factors form the structure of the transferability assessment:

- Population context
- Sector specific context
- Political context
- Economic context

Each contextual factor comprises several indicators to guide the decision-making process. Indicators are divided into two groups: 1) *existing indicators* – indicators with readily available sources of data; and 2) *new indicators* – indicators that require collection of new data for example through surveys, site visits and/or discussions with key contacts from the owner setting (Barnfield, Savolainen and Lounamaa, 2020[54]).

The transferability assessment framework is applicable to both intra- and inter-country transfers. The former relates to transfers within a country, for example, expanding an intervention to new schools within the same district. When compared to inter-country transfers, intra-country transfers are generally simpler given the owner and target setting are more likely to be similar (e.g. language, culture, education levels, and organisation of the health care system).

Given the attributes of transferability are specific to an intervention, policy makers should view the indicators outlined in this step as a reference point only (Wang, Moss and Hiller, 2006[52]). That is, **policy makers should adapt the transferability assessment to suit their needs by adding/removing indicators as necessary.** For example, indicators to measure health information system maturity are not relevant for assessing school-based obesity interventions. In addition, **the extent of the transferability assessment will depend on available resources** (both time and financial).

1.3.1. Preliminary review of the best practice owner setting

An understanding of the owner setting is an important first step within the transferral process (European Commission, 2015[55]; CHRODIS, 2017[56]). It involves obtaining information from those involved in designing, implementing and/or evaluating the intervention. For example, through study visits, special training sessions and/or short-term exchanges (European Commission, 2015[55]). If this is not possible (e.g. due to budgetary constraints), policy makers in the target setting can reach out using digital methods.

A preliminary review provides policy makers in the target setting with an opportunity to obtain information not readily available through public sources. Questions policy makers could ask include:

- Has the intervention been transferred to another setting? If so, are there materials on how to transfer the intervention? (see Box 1.9 for two case studies)
- What are the core components of the intervention? (i.e. components critical to achieve desired outcomes)[3]
- Was there a local "champion" or "champions" responsible for driving change?
- What partnerships and alliances did the intervention rely on for success?

A preliminary review may also be useful for collecting information on primary source indicators listed in Section 1.3.2.

Box 1.9. Case study: EUPAP and the Whole Grain Partnership – existing transferal material

The Prescription of Physical Activity (PAP) and Whole Grain Partnership have both been identified as best practice interventions in their owner setting – i.e. Sweden and Denmark, respectively. As a result, both interventions are in the process of being transferred to other EU Member States.

Prescription of Physical Activity (PAP) (Sweden)

PAP is a primary-care based intervention where general practitioners (GPs) provide patients with individualised written prescriptions to boost physical activity levels using latest scientific knowledge.

Following the success of PAP in Sweden, a three-year project was initiated to facilitate the transfer and adoption of the intervention to ten EU member states (EUPAP). As part of the project a Feasibility Study Guide was developed to assist policy makers in the target setting assess their overall "preparedness of practice transfer". The Guide is broken into two components:

- **Early diagnosis** (macro level): identifies political priorities, current and past experiences with physical activity prescription programs, and legal and financial issues.
- **Preparedness for implementation** (micro level): defines the stakeholders involved during implementation and the social, cultural and political context in which they operate. In addition, characteristics of the health care setting PAP will be implemented are identified, as well as who will implement (e.g. health care professionals) and receive PAP services.

A copy of the Feasibility Study Guide is available here: https://www.eupap.org/public-documents.

The Danish Whole Grain Partnership (Denmark)

The Danish Whole Grain Partnership is a public-private partnership between various organisations including government and food companies. The overall objective of the partnership is to increase whole grain intake, which it achieves by allowing partnering organisations to use a front-of-pack, easy-to-understand whole grain logo.

> The Whole Grain Partnership is considered one of the world's most successful interventions to boost whole grain consumption (Suthers, Broom and Beck, 2018[57]). Consequently in 2019 the WholeEUGrain three-year project was launched to facilitate the transfer of the intervention from Denmark to Romania, Slovenia, and Bosnia and Herzegovina. The project developed two outputs to assist countries transfer and implement the intervention:
>
> - **Preparedness and feasibility study**: a report to assist countries assess whether they are prepared to implement the intervention.
> - **ToolBox**: a guide to help policy makers successfully implement the Whole Grain Partnership in their local setting (available here: https://www.gzs.si/wholeugrain/vsebina/Publications#1150561284-reports).
>
> In addition to the Feasibility Study and ToolBox, there is a "summer school" which offers training to those interested in transferring the Whole Grain Partnership to their local setting.

Developing a relationship between best practice owners is not only important at the start of the transfer process, but also during the transfer and implementation stage, as described in Box 1.10. If best practice owners and implementers agree to work together, at the outset, both parties should agree on the "nature of the transfer" (i.e. an exact or loose replication of the intervention) (Stegeman et al., 2020[58]).

> ### Box 1.10. Case study: CHRODIS PLUS Joint Action (the Netherlands and Ireland) – creating a good relationship between best practice owners and implementers
>
> In 2020, the Joint Action on Chronic Diseases (CHRODIS-PLUS Joint Action) produced a report outlining recommendations for transferring and implementing good practice interventions. The report outlines five recommendations including an investment between project "owners" and "implementers" in all phases of the intervention (Stegeman et al., 2020[58]). As noted by the authors, "even if a good practice is thoroughly described, regular support may be needed from the initial developers, to help maintain the integrity of the core elements that made it a success" (Stegeman et al., 2020[58]). Real-world examples from the Joint Action are summarised below.
>
> **JOGG (Young People at a Healthy Weight)**
>
> JOGG is a Dutch public health intervention that aims to improve diet and physical activity amongst young people (0-19 years). Activities within JOGG are decided at the local (municipal/city) level, for example, drinking water initiatives in kindergartens and creating playgrounds for children.
>
> Iceland, in an effort to further develop its existing Health Promoting Community (HPC) programme, chose to transfer elements of the JOGG intervention. The transfer was seen as successful in part due to the "valuable support provided by the JOGG programme" (Gunnarsdóttir and Ingibjörg, 2020[59]). For example, the original site visit to the Netherlands allowed Icelandic officials to get an in-depth understanding of JOGG as well as develop casual ties with the JOGG programme. Further, throughout the transfer and implementation process, representatives from JOGG were generous in providing materials and time (e.g. regular phone meetings and emails) (Gunnarsdóttir and Ingibjörg, 2020[59]).
>
> **Active School Flag**
>
> The Active Flag (ASF) is a school-based intervention that aims to improve levels of physical activity amongst children aged five to 18 years. ASF was originally developed in Ireland and was subsequently transferred to two schools in the Piedmont region of Italy and the Klaipeda District Municipality in Lithuania.

> Two site visits were undertaken as part of the transfer process: 1) a visit to Ireland by Italian implementers to learn more about ASF before it was transferred; and 2) a visit by Irish good practice owners to Italy once the intervention was implemented to share experiences and receive feedback. In addition, throughout the implementation process, officials in Ireland and Italy communicated regularly through emails and a closed Facebook group. The regular communication between Irish and Italian officials was viewed as a key success factor (Stegeman et al., 2020[58]).

1.3.2. Comparing the best practice owner and target setting

To assess transferability, this guidebook recommends policy makers compare the best practice owner setting and target setting against the following four contextual factors: population, sector specific, political and economic contexts.

The ideal setting for the best practice intervention isn't necessarily that of the best practice owner. Further, indicator values may not be available for the owner setting. In these instances, policy makers should instead assess whether the target setting is receptive to the best practice intervention based on the indicator.

Population context

The "population context" refers to population characteristics and covers sociodemographic factors as well as broader cultural considerations (see Table 1.6).

Table 1.6. Population context indicators

Population context indicators		
The following population characteristics are the same or similar in the best practice owner and target setting **OR** the target setting is receptive to the intervention based on the indicator	Yes	No
Existing indicators		
Population health needs	☐	☐
Age structure	☐	☐
Race/ethnicity structure	☐	☐
Level of education	☐	☐
Level of health literacy	☐	☐
New indicators		
Public acceptability	☐	☐
Public cultural norms and expectations	☐	☐

Source: JA-CHRODIS (2017[60]), "Joint Action on Chronic Diseases and Promoting Healthy Ageing across the Life Cycle (JA-CHRODIS). Work Package 5: Good practices in the field of health promotion and chronic disease prevention across the life cycle. Recommendations report on applicability", http://chrodis.eu/wp-content/uploads/2014October_170223_wp5-t5_report-successfactorstransf-scalability_wotable2.pdf; Schloemer and Schröder-Bäck (2018[49]), "Criteria for evaluating transferability of health interventions: a systematic review and thematic synthesis", https://doi.org/10.1186/s13012-018-0751-8; Wang, Moss and Hiller (2006[52]), "Applicability and transferability of interventions in evidence-based public health", https://doi.org/10.1093/heapro/dai025; WHO (2011[61]), "Identifying and addressing barriers to implementing policy options. In: SURE guides for preparing and using evidence-based policy briefs", https://epoc.cochrane.org/sites/epoc.cochrane.org/files/public/uploads/SURE-Guides-v2.1/Collectedfiles/sure_guides.html; Kidholm et al. (2012[62]), "A model for assessment of telemedicine applications: Mast", https://doi.org/10.1017/S0266462311000638; Cuijpers, De Graaf and Bohlmeijer (2005[63]), "Adapting and disseminating effective public health interventions in another country: Towards a systematic approach", https://doi.org/10.1093/eurpub/cki124.

It is important to first understand whether the intervention is suitable for addressing population health needs in the target setting. For example, by analysing key population health trends across different population sub-groups, as well as levels of unmet need (Ng and de Colombani, 2015[2]; CHRODIS, 2017[56]; Schloemer and Schröder-Bäck, 2018[49]; Bonell et al., 2006[64]). This assessment should be undertaken early on given it is a pre-requisite for evidence-based decision-making (Yost et al., 2014[65]) and intervention effectiveness (Bonell et al., 2006[64]). Other population characteristics to consider may include levels of health literacy, education as well as the ethnic structure of the population as this can affect the success of an intervention, for example, intervention take-up.

In addition to examining existing indicators on population characteristics, policy makers are encouraged to collect information to assess public acceptability of the intervention as well as cultural norms and expectations, for reasons described below.

Public acceptability: Public acceptability refers to perception among the public that an intervention is agreeable, palatable, or satisfactory. It therefore reflects several concepts including (Sekhon, Cartwright and Francis, 2017[66]; WHO, 2011[61]):

- Whether the intervention is socially, culturally, philosophically and ethically accepted
- Whether the intervention is seen to address key health needs within the population
- Whether the intervention is seen as the most appropriate response to addressing health needs
- The burden associated with participating in the intervention
- The extent to which the public understand the intervention.

Policy makers are less likely to implement an intervention if it does not receive support from the public (or is met by public resistance) (Stok et al., 2016[67]; Diepeveen et al., 2013[68]).

Relative to indicators such as age/gender structure of the population and education levels, the level of public acceptability may be difficult to measure. Suggested methods to measure public acceptability include questionnaires and focus groups (Saracutu et al., 2018[69]; Stok et al., 2016[67]).

Public cultural norms and expectations: culture is a set of "distinctive spiritual, material, intellectual and emotional features" within a society which determine values, traditions and beliefs (Napier et al., 2017[70]). It is therefore not limited to national, race, ethnic or religious factors (Napier et al., 2017[70]; Napier et al., 2014[71]).

The impact of the cultural context is growing increasingly important in understanding the success or failure of health care interventions (WHO Regional Office for Europe, n.d.[72]). Therefore, it is important policy makers compare cultural differences between the owner and target setting (Iwelunmor, Newsome and Airhihenbuwa, 2014[73]). Failing to do so may result in wasted resources as well as widening existing health inequalities (Napier et al., 2014[71]).

Useful databases: Population context

OECD Statistics. OECD provides national level statistics across a range of topics including statistics on population structure. https://stats.oecd.org/.

Eurostat. Eurostat provides comparative data for European countries across a range of topics including "population and social conditions". https://ec.europa.eu/eurostat/data/database.

Eurobarometer surveys. Eurobarometer surveys collect information from public opinion surveys across all EU Member States. https://www.europarl.europa.eu/at-your-service/en/be-heard/eurobarometer.

WHO Global Health Observatory. The WHO publishes data on a wide-range of population health indicators for countries across the world. https://www.who.int/data/gho/data/indicators.

Institute for Health Metrics and Evaluation (IHME). IHME provides publically available data on the burden of disease across a range of countries, which is useful for measuring population health needs. http://www.healthdata.org/.

Sector specific context

The "sector specific context" refers to governance/regulation, financing, workforce, capital (including technological infrastructure) and access arrangements in the sector the intervention will operate (see Table 1.7). Given the breadth of public health interventions, this may include sectors such as health, education, environment, transport and housing.

Table 1.7. Sector specific context indicators

Sector specific context indicators		
The following sector characteristics are the same or similar in the best practice owner and target setting **OR** the target setting is receptive to the intervention based on the indicator	Yes	No
Existing indicators		
Governance / regulation		
Organisational structure of the sector	☐	☐
Regulations and legislation governing the sector	☐	☐
Financing		
Remuneration system for service providers	☐	☐
Workforce		
Workforce volume (per capita)	☐	☐
Workforce skills	☐	☐
Capital resources		
Land / space	☐	☐
Facilities	☐	☐
Equipment	☐	☐
Digital and technological infrastructure	☐	☐
Access		
Financial access	☐	☐
Geographical access	☐	☐
New indicators		
Workforce		
Workforce (and other stakeholder) acceptability	☐	☐
Existing interventions		
Compatible / synergistic interventions	☐	☐
Competing interventions	☐	☐

Source: Barnfield, Savolainen and Lounamaa (2020[54]), "Health Promotion Interventions: Lessons from the Transfer of Good Practices in CHRODIS-PLUS", https://doi.org/10.3390/ijerph17041281; WHO (2011[61]), "Identifying and addressing barriers to implementing policy options. In: SURE guides for preparing and using evidence-based policy briefs", https://epoc.cochrane.org/sites/epoc.cochrane.org/files/public/uploads/SURE-Guides-v2.1/Collectedfiles/sure_guides.html; Kidholm et al. (2012[62]), "A model for assessment of telemedicine applications: Mast", https://doi.org/10.1017/S0266462311000638; Cuijpers, De Graaf and Bohlmeijer (2005[63]), "Adapting and disseminating effective public health interventions in another country: Towards a systematic approach", https://doi.org/10.1093/eurpub/cki124; Schloemer and Schröder-Bäck (2018[49]), "Criteria for evaluating transferability of health interventions: a systematic review and thematic synthesis", https://doi.org/10.1186/s13012-018-0751-8; Wang, Moss and Hiller (2006[52]), "Applicability and transferability of interventions in evidence-based public health", https://doi.org/10.1093/heapro/dai025; McCannn, Schall and Perla (2008[74]), "Planning for Scale: A Guide for Designing Large-Scale Improvement Initiatives. IHI Innovation Series white paper", www.IHI.org.

Governance: governance reflects key players who develop and implement key strategic policies to achieve policy objectives, as well regulate the behaviour of stakeholders (e.g. payers and providers) (WHO, n.d.[75]). An assessment of differences in governance arrangements may be relevant, for example, if the success of an intervention depends on local decision-making power. In the health sector, governance arrangements are particularly important when considering transferring an integrated care intervention (Box 1.11).

> **Box 1.11. Case study: Oulu's digital Self Care Service (Finland) – governance and transferability**
>
> "Self Care Service" is an electronic online platform available to the citizens of the City of Oulu, Finland. The platforms offers a range of free online services to enable integrated care, such as: online appointment booking; online support for urgent health issues; ePrescriptions; primary care appointments; home monitoring; and information on health prevention, amongst other things.
>
> The Self Care Service has been transferred to other municipalities in Finland, but not to other countries. Transferring the necessary IT is not seen as a barrier to implementing the intervention, rather, it is the organisation of the health care system in regard to how services are funded and reimbursed as well as how primary health care centres and hospitals are organised (Lupiañez-Villanueva, Sachinopoulou and Thebe, 2015[76]). Further, for the intervention to be successfully transferred, technological innovation should be aligned with the organisation of the health care system (Lupiañez-Villanueva, Sachinopoulou and Thebe, 2015[76]).

Financing (reimbursement mechanisms): reimbursement systems offer incentives and can therefore drive professional/provider behaviour (e.g. fee-for-service, pay-for-performance, budgets, capitation salaries, or mixed models) (Tao, Agerholm and Burström, 2016[77]). A comparison of reimbursement mechanisms is important to see whether professional/provider motivation differs in the target setting (WHO, 2011[61]). For example, an intervention designed to boost services for multimorbid patients may work in a setting where providers receive risk-adjusted payments (which compensate for higher treatment costs) and fail in a setting where providers receive lump-sum payment for all services.

Workforce: comparing the volume (per capita) and skills of the workforce will determine whether the target setting has the capacity to operate the intervention or whether additional human resources and/or training are necessary (Schloemer and Schröder-Bäck, 2018[49]; Cuijpers, De Graaf and Bohlmeijer, 2005[63]; Wang, Moss and Hiller, 2006[52]). For example, a key barrier to implementing Active School Flag (a school-based physical activity intervention) from Ireland to Italy was teacher confidence due to their lack of training in physical education (Stegeman et al., 2020[58]).

It is also important to assess the workforce and broader stakeholder acceptability of the intervention as this will determine "buy-in" (e.g. is the intervention the most appropriate action for addressing a recognised health care need?) (WHO, 2011[61]; Cuijpers, De Graaf and Bohlmeijer, 2005[63]; Barnfield, Savolainen and Lounamaa, 2020[54]).[4] For example, a chronic care wound management intervention developed as part of CHRODIS-PLUS Joint Action, in part, credited its success to the readiness for change amongst the medical profession who recognised the need to change the organisation of care. For another example, see Box 1.12.

> **Box 1.12. Case study: ToyBox (Scotland) – measuring acceptability**
>
> ToyBox is a Kindergarten-based intervention aimed at promoting healthy lifestyles to prevent overweight and obesity rates among children. The intervention is delivered by teachers over a 24-week period, which concentrates on the four main energy balance-related behaviours: water consumption; healthy snacking; physical activity; and sedentary behaviour.

> To assess the acceptability of implementing ToyBox, feedback was collected from preschool practitioners and parents. For preschool practitioners, this involved focus groups where participants were invited to discuss barriers and facilitators to implementing the intervention and the use of an RCT for evaluation. Parents, conversely, participated in one-on-one semi-structured interviews to discuss barriers/facilitators for delivering the home component of the intervention (each parent received a GBP 25 (USD PPP (purchasing power parity) 37) shopping voucher as an incentive) (Malden et al., 2020[78]).

Capital resources: capital resources are the physical assets required to implement and deliver an intervention. These cover long-term assets including land, facilities (usually stationary sites where services are provided such as buildings), equipment (machines, tools or objects), and digital and technical infrastructure, for example, to support eHealth (Box 1.13). Example capital resources include health information system technology, number of cooking facilities available to schoolchildren, gym facilities, and land space (e.g. for playgrounds or public transport). Understanding capital resources in both settings is important for determining the cost of implementing the intervention, as discussed under "economic context".

> **Box 1.13. Case study: SCIROCCO Maturity Model – eHealth readiness for integrated care**
>
> Scaling Integrated Care in Context (SCIROCCO) is a project co-funded by the European Commission which aims to adopt and transfer good practices in integrated care. A key output of SCIRICCO is the Maturity Model which outlines 12 dimensions necessary for assessing areas of strength for implementing integrated care, as well as gaps (SCIROCCO, n.d.[79]).
>
> One of the Maturity Model's dimensions is "information & eHealth services" and is scored based on a six-point scale (from least ready to most ready) (SCIROCCO, n.d.[79]):
>
> - There are no eHealth services to support integrated care in place (score: 0)
> - There is recognition of need but there is no strategy and/or plan on how to deploy eHealth services to support integrated care (score: 1)
> - There is a mandate and plan(s) to deploy regional/national eHealth services across the health care system but not yet implemented (score: 2)
> - eHealth services to support integrated care are piloted but there is no yet region wide coverage (score: 3)
> - eHealth services to support integrated care are deployed widely at a large scale (score: 4)
> - Universal, at-scale regional/national eHealth services used by all integrated care stakeholders (score: 5).
>
> EHealth readiness scores from the owner setting are used to assist policy makers in the target setting determine whether their eHealth system is mature enough.

Access: key factors to consider when comparing the owner and target setting include differences in geographic, virtual and financial accessibility for eligible individuals. Geographical and virtual access refers to a population's ability to physically and virtually (i.e. telemedicine) access services, respectively, with those living in regional/remote areas and/or on low-income particularly vulnerable (Rice and Smith, 2001[80]). Financial access refers to the absence of cost barriers to access an intervention. Costs barriers include out-of-pocket payments (OOPs) such as co-payments, co-insurance and deductibles, as well as hidden costs such as transport (Brooks, Wilson and Amir, 2011[81]).

Existing interventions: existing interventions in the target setting may affect the success of a new best practice intervention (Cuijpers, De Graaf and Bohlmeijer, 2005[63]; Cambon et al., 2013[82]; Burchett,

Umoquit and Dobrow, 2011[51]). Existing interventions with the same objective may overlap with the best practice intervention leading to duplication, or may be antagonistic and work against the intervention's objectives. Conversely, they may have a synergistic effect leading to positive outcomes, for example, through existing infrastructure, networks and a workforce with relevant skills. In fact, findings from the CHRODIS-PLUS Joint Action recommend policy makers "build on existing good practice" (Stegeman et al., 2020[58]). Further, existing interventions with similar objectives can create a culture conducive to the success to the best practice intervention. For example, the more "established the culture of HPDP [health promotion and disease prevention], the greater the incentive for professionals at all levels to invest their time and energy in relevant activities" (Stegeman et al., 2020[58]). (See Box 1.14 for an example on how existing interventions in the target setting can have a positive effect.).

> **Box 1.14. Case study: Active School Flag (transfer from Ireland to Italy and Lithuania) – impact of existing interventions**
>
> Active School Flag is a school-based intervention which aims to improve levels of physical activity amongst children aged between 4 and 12. The intervention was originally developed in Ireland where it is active in approximately 800 schools.
>
> The success of Active School Flag in Ireland led to its transfer to the Piedmont region in Italy and the Klaipėda city and Klaipėda district municipalities in Lithuania. Barnfield et al. (2020) noted that implementation of the Active School Flag intervention in Italy and Lithuania benefited from previous interventions, which had created an environment supportive of health-promoting initiatives in school. For example, it was easier to identify qualified implementers as well as train new implementers (Barnfield, Savolainen and Lounamaa, 2020[54]).
>
>> *"The use of a good practice to expand (or 'mesh with') a current programme aids transfer and implementation"*, (Barnfield, Savolainen and Lounamaa, 2020[54]).
>
>> *"It was easier for localities that already had a strong foundation in health promotion and disease prevention to trail the new initiatives."*, (Stegeman et al., 2020[58]).

Useful databases: Sector context (health system-level)

OECD Health Statistics. OECD Health Statistics provides comparable data on topics such as health system financing, governance, workforce, utilisation and status. http://www.oecd.org/els/health-systems/health-data.htm. (Pre-prepared statistics comparing countries across various health dimensions can be found in the following OECD publications: *Health at a Glance: Europe 2018* and *Health at a Glance 2019* (OECD/European Union, 2018[83]; OECD, 2019[84])).

OECD Health Systems Characteristic survey. OECD has created an interactive tool allowing users to compare health system characteristics (e.g. governance, delivery and resource allocation) across all 35 member countries, 2 key partnering countries and 21 Latin-American countries. The latest available information for OECD countries is from 2016. https://www.oecd.org/els/health-systems/characteristics.htm.

WHO Global Health Observatory: the WHO publishes data on a wide-range of health indicators for countries across the world. https://www.who.int/data/gho/data/indicators.

Eurostat. Eurostat provides comparable information on a range of health indicators including care, expenditure and resources across European countries. https://ec.europa.eu/eurostat/data/database.

European Observatory for Health Systems and Policies. The Observatory publish a range of material on country health systems reviews and country health profiles. https://www.hspm.org/searchandcompare.aspx.

The Commonwealth Fund. The Fund is a privately run foundation designed to promote better performing health care systems. The Fund provides free-to-access international profiles of health care systems. https://www.commonwealthfund.org/international-health-policy-center/countries.

Political context

The "political context" refers to political will from key decision-makers to implement the intervention (see Table 1.8).

Table 1.8. Political context indicators

Political context indicators		
The following political characteristics are the same or similar in the best practice owner and target setting **OR** the target setting is receptive to the intervention based on the indicator	Yes	No
Existing indicators		
The intervention aligns with policy priorities at the relevant level of government	☐	☐
The intervention aligns with policy strategies and/or action plans at the relevant level of government	☐	☐
New indicators		
The intervention has received political support from key decision-makers	☐	☐
The intervention has received political commitment from key decision-makers	☐	☐
Support from key stakeholder groups	☐	☐
Established connection between decision-makers and stakeholders	☐	☐

Source: Cuijpers, De Graaf and Bohlmeijer (2005[63]), "Adapting and disseminating effective public health interventions in another country: Towards a systematic approach", https://doi.org/10.1093/eurpub/cki124; Wang, Moss and Hiller (2006[52]), "Applicability and transferability of interventions in evidence-based public health", https://doi.org/10.1093/heapro/dai025; JA-CHRODIS (2017[60]), "Joint Action on Chronic Diseases and Promoting Healthy Ageing across the Life Cycle (JA-CHRODIS). Work Package 5: Good practices in the field of health promotion and chronic disease prevention across the life cycle. Recommendations report on applicability", http://chrodis.eu/wp-content/uploads/2014October_170223_wp5-t5_report-successfactorstransf-scalability_wotable2.pdf; Schloemer and Schröder-Bäck (2018[49]), "Criteria for evaluating transferability of health interventions: a systematic review and thematic synthesis", https://doi.org/10.1186/s13012-018-0751-8;; WHO (2011[61]), "Identifying and addressing barriers to implementing policy options. In: SURE guides for preparing and using evidence-based policy briefs", https://epoc.cochrane.org/sites/epoc.cochrane.org/files/public/uploads/SURE-Guides-v2.1/Collectedfiles/sure_guides.html; National Collaborating Centre for Methods and Tools (2007[85]), "Tool for Assessing Applicability and Transferability of Evidence", https://www.nccmt.ca/uploads/media/media/0001/01/a13748201ebe5a6793cc641b109e21c70307dfdc.pdf.

Governments today face tight budgetary constraints concurrent with growing demand for services to meet population needs. The health sector, therefore, increasingly "competes" with itself and other sectors for political priority (WHO; ExpandNet, 2009[86]).

In order to secure political support, it is important that interventions align with overarching political priorities, strategies and action plans (Frieden, 2014[87]; McCannon, Schall and Perla, 2008[74]). These may include priorities/strategies/action plans at the international level, such as the United Nations Sustainable Development Goals (SDGs), or at the national level, for example, alcohol, obesity prevention or physical activity strategies. Political support is essential as it leads to the provision of resources needed to "co-ordinate, implement and sustain" an intervention (see Box 1.15 for a case study on the benefits of having political support) (Frieden, 2014[87]).

Political support is particularly important for public health interventions given they affect multiple sectors, both public and private, and sometimes face opposition from certain interest groups (Frieden, 2014[87]). A prime example is opposition from industry, which often has access to significant financial resources to fund lobbying efforts, which can result in "undue influence" on public policy decisions (OECD, 2014[88]). Further, the benefits of public health interventions, although large on a population-wide scale, are generally small for each individual and not felt immediately (Rose, Khaw and Marmot, 2008[89]). This leads to a misperception over the benefits associated with the intervention thereby reducing public support (Rose, Khaw and Marmot, 2008[89]).

> **Box 1.15. Case study: Multimodal Training Intervention (transfer to Lithuania) – the importance of political support**
>
> The Klaipėda district and Klaipėda city municipalities in Lithuania transferred Iceland's Multimodal Training Intervention – a nutritional education and physical exercise programme targeting those aged 65 years and over.
>
> The development of MTI in Lithuania required support from the Ministry of Health of the Republic of Lithuania, the Hygiene Institute, Public Health Offices and municipal leaders and administrative staff. In their evaluation report, officials from Lithuania noted that participation from these key political bodies was essential, therefore, any future transfers should involve political decision-makers from the outset (Stegeman et al., 2020[58]).
>
> Positive outcomes achieved by MTI in Lithuania led the Klaipeda District Municipality to develop a physical activity Act making it easier for similar interventions to be implemented in the future (Stegeman et al., 2020[58]).

Useful databases: Political context

WHO Global Health Observatory: the WHO publishes data on countries with national action plans and strategies for different health issues (e.g. diabetes, unhealthy diet, physical activity). https://www.who.int/data/gho/data/indicators.

Eurostat. Eurostat provides comparable information for European countries on EU policy. https://ec.europa.eu/eurostat/data/database.

European Observatory for Health Systems and Policies. The Observatory includes a tool to readily access and compare information on current and future health reforms and policies across a range of countries. https://www.hspm.org/searchandcompare.aspx.

Economic context

The "economic context" aims to assess whether the intervention is affordable in the target setting (Table 1.9).

Table 1.9. Economic context indicators

Economic context indicators	Yes	No
The following economic characteristics are the same or similar in the best practice owner and target setting OR the target setting is receptive to the intervention based on the indicator		
Existing indicators		
GDP (or GNI) per capita	☐	☐
Income per capita	☐	☐
Current account balance	☐	☐
Public and private debt ratio	☐	☐
Proportion of GDP spent on health	☐	☐
Health spending per capita	☐	☐
Health expenditure by type of service (e.g. public health)	☐	☐
New indicator		
Cost of implementing and operating the intervention*	☐	☐

Note: *Discussed further below.
Source: Kidholm et al. (2012[62]), "A model for assessment of telemedicine applications: Mast", https://doi.org/10.1017/S0266462311000638; WHO (2011[61]), "Identifying and addressing barriers to implementing policy options. In: SURE guides for preparing and using evidence-based policy briefs", https://epoc.cochrane.org/sites/epoc.cochrane.org/files/public/uploads/SURE-Guides-v2.1/Collectedfiles/sure_guides.html; Cambon et al. (2013[82]), "A tool to analyse the transferablity of health promotion interventions", https://doi.org/10.1186/1471-2458-13-1184; OECD (2020[90]), "Main Economic Indicators (MEI)", https://www.oecd.org/sdd/oecdmaineconomicindicatorsmei.htm; OECD (2019[91]), "Health expenditure and financing", https://stats.oecd.org/Index.aspx?DataSetCode=SHA#.

Long-term affordability plays a critical role in determining whether an intervention can be successfully transferred. Several indicators to assess the economic context of the owner and target setting are availability such as GDP, GNI (gross national income) and health expenditure per capita (see Table 1.9, "existing indicators"). These indicators are recorded at the national level and therefore may be of limited use if assessing the transferability of a local intervention that is not representative of the entire country.

It is therefore important for policy makers to undertake a more in-depth evaluation of implementation and operating costs in the owner and target setting as these will likely differ. A high-level, three-stage process for assessing the cost of an intervention is provided below:

- First, develop an understanding of the financial costs associated with implementing and operating the best practice intervention in the owner setting (e.g. working time of health professionals and physical infrastructure needs). Information about these costs may be publically available (e.g. from an economic evaluation report) or may require discussions/visits with intervention leads in the owner setting (e.g. during the preliminary review stage).
- Second, assess whether financial costs are likely to be similar in the owner and target setting. For example, the implementation cost of a digital health intervention will differ depending on whether necessary technical infrastructure already exists (Kidholm et al., 2012[92]).
- Information from stages 1 and 2 are necessary for stage 3, which involves assessing whether the intervention is affordable in the target setting (e.g. by comparing costs with available budget) (RE-AIM, 2020[11]).

Further details on costing an intervention can be found in Step 2 (Implement) – page 52 ("Assessing resource needs against existing capacity and readiness").

Useful databases: Economic context

OECD Economy Statistics. OECD Statistics provides a wide range of comparable economic data across countries. https://data.oecd.org/economy.htm.

World Bank (World Development Indicators): the World Bank has developed a databank providing information on a range of economic indicators. https://data.worldbank.org/indicator (see "Economy and Growth").

Eurostat. Eurostat provides a range of comparable economic statistics for European countries. https://ec.europa.eu/eurostat/data/database.

Indicators used to measure transferability will depend on various factors such as the intervention, the owner and target setting, and resources available to undertake the transferability assessment. Box 1.16 provides an example transferability assessment to demonstrate how the framework proposed by OECD can be adapted to suit the specific needs of policy makers. Specifically, it presents a list of indicators relevant for assessing whether an mHealth intervention offering personalised nutrition can be transferred to another setting.

Box 1.16. Case study: Let Food Be Your Medicine (mHealth app) – transferability assessment

The transferability assessment below refers to is a web-based and mobile app providing consumers with personalised nutrition (PN) advice – Let Food Be Your Medicine. Nutritional advice is based on a consumer's dietary intake (and genetic tests, if provided) compared to recommended levels outlined by the European Food Safety Agency. The app is designed for both preventive and treatment purposes and can cost up between EUR 0-5/month (USD PPP 0-7.3), depending on application features.

Population context

- Is this an appropriate intervention? Does the public accept this type of digital intervention? (e.g. are they an appropriate response high obesity rates? Does the public understand the intervention and its purpose?)
- Does the population trust their personal health information will be used, stored and managed appropriately?
- What proportion of the population have access to the internet?
- What proportion of the population have access to a smartphone?
- What are the rates of digital health literacy?

Intervention-specific context (digital health)

- What, if any, existing web-based / mHealth apps are currently available to the population?
- How accepted is the use mHealth apps to improve diet amongst health care professionals?
- How accepted is the concept of personalised nutrition to improve diets amongst health care professionals?
- Are there any other online nutrition tools available to the population?
- What are the regulations/legislation regarding the use of genetic information?

> **Political context**
> - Does the intervention align with policy strategies and/or action plans at the relevant level of government?
> - Is there political support and commitment from key decision-makers?
>
> **Economic context**
> - What is the cost of implementing the intervention in the target setting (e.g. how do infrastructure costs differ between the owner and target setting?)
> - What is the GDP per capita in the population?
> - What is the average disposable income of individuals/families?

1.3.3. Acting on transferability assessment results

The transferability assessment will lead to one of three possible outcomes:

1. Transfer the intervention in its original form
2. Transfer an adapted version of the intervention to suit the needs of the population
3. Do not transfer and return to Step 1a.

The owner and target setting do not have to be identical for an intervention to be transferred successfully. Changes to an intervention may be necessary to ensure it is sustainable, culturally appropriate or more widely accessible (Schloemer and Schröder-Bäck, 2018[49]; Movsisyan et al., 2019[93]; Escoffery et al., 2018[94]). Alternatively, changes to the target setting may be necessary for it to be receptive of the intervention (e.g. training for staff to ensure they have the skills to deliver the intervention) (Wang, Moss and Hiller, 2006[52]).

The more complex an intervention, the more likely it will need to be adapted to suit the target setting. Integrated care interventions, for instance, are often adapted given they bring together different health care payers and providers whose mutual relationships differ greatly across countries/regions (see Box 1.17 for a case study on the importance of adapting interventions to suit the target setting).

> **Box 1.17. Case study: Digital health transformation of integrated care in Europe – adapting financing methods**
>
> SELFIE (sustainable integrated care models for multimorbidity, delivery, financing and performance) is an EU-funded Horizon project designed to improve integrated care for people with multimorbidity. As part of the project, 13 practical transferability recommendations were developed, including recommendations regarding the "transferability of financing methods" (Kaló et al., 2020[95]).
>
> Transferability recommendations related to financing clearly note that "transferability of financing methods is not a mandatory condition for transferring integrated care models from other jurisdictions" (Kaló et al., 2020[95]). As a first step, it is recommended policy makers explore whether the financing method used in the owner setting can be adapted to the target setting. If the financing method is neither transferable nor adaptable, a new financing methodology should be developed that aligns with the target setting (Kaló et al., 2020[95]).

1.3.4. Designing the evaluation study

By the end of Step 1, policy makers should have identified a best practice intervention suitable for transfer to the target setting. Prior to implementing the best practice intervention, it is important to design an evaluation study. Designing the evaluation study at an early stage is necessary as it specifies the indicators and therefore the data needed to undertake an evaluation. Importantly, this includes identifying effectiveness indicators (also referred to as outcome indicators), which may be universal (see Box 1.3) or intervention specific (see Annex B).

For the purposes of this guidebook, **details on how to design an evaluation study are discussed in Step 3**, alongside details on how to execute an evaluation.

1.4. Conclusion of Step 1

The first step of the guidebook is designed to assist policy makers identify best practice public health interventions. Based on a review of the literature, previous MCDA frameworks and expert feedback, five criteria were deemed necessary for making this decision: effectiveness, efficiency, equity, evidence-base, and extent of coverage. A best practice intervention shouldn't automatically be considered appropriate for implementation in a new setting. Therefore, it is important to assess the transferability of a best practice intervention by comparing the best practice owner and target setting covering dimensions such as political and economic feasibility.

The framework for identifying and assessing the transferability of best practice interventions is designed to cover a range of public health interventions. For this reason, **it is important that policy makers adapt the framework to suit their specific needs**. This will involve adding/removing indicators from the best practice criteria as well as the transferability assessment.

Once a public health intervention has been identified as best practice and transferable, the next step is implementation, which is discussed in Step 2 of the guidebook.

Step 2. Implement

This section of the guidebook helps policy makers understand the process of implementation and highlights the need for a formal implementation process to successfully transfer a best practice intervention to a target setting. It provides a general framework for understanding implementation and helps policy makers, who select and fund interventions but do usually not implement them, a guide for assessing whether implementation is sufficiently addressed in the planned transfer of the intervention. It also suggests ways in which implementation can be monitored.

The section assumes that a transferability assessment (as described in Step 1b, Section 1.3) has been completed and that the result of this assessment is that the intervention is transferable to the target setting in its original or adapted form.

2.1. Introduction to implementing an intervention

2.1.1. The need for structured implementation

Interventions to prevent or manage key public health issues are complex. As discussed in Step 1b (Section 1.3), they involve several interacting components, often target heterogeneous populations and interact with their context. They are usually delivered by people who are part of established health or social care organisations and they may be supported by technical tools, including information and communications technology. Crucially, to achieve their desired effects on relevant health outcomes, they often aim to create an interplay between their individual components to change the behaviour of health and social care providers and enhance the delivery of services, to inform the population or patient group targeted, and, ultimately, change the behaviour of citizens and patients. While research is constantly identifying many possible ways of improving population health, for instance through changing living environments and personal behaviours, these changes do not usually occur automatically to benefit populations. Many advances are not put into practice adequately, often because the will, or skill, to change behaviour are missing (Jenkins, 2003[96]).

Because such interventions rely on the interactions of many people, tools and processes, they only succeed if these interactions are co-ordinated through careful implementation. While appropriate selection and adaptation of interventions (as discussed in Step 1a (Section 1.2) and Step 1b (Section 1.3) are prerequisites for achieving intended outcomes, these steps on their own are insufficient to ensure success. Even an appropriate and well-designed intervention can fail if it is poorly implemented. Many studies have shown that factors related to implementation affect the outcomes achieved by health promotion and prevention interventions (see, for instance, Durlak and DuPre (2008[97]) or Nielsen (2015[98])).

For the purpose of this guidebook, implementation generally refers to "the process of putting to use or integrating evidence-based interventions within a setting" (Brownson et al., 2015, p. 305[99]). Specifically, this section guides policy makers in ensuring that interventions identified as best practice (Step 1a, Section 1.2) and suitable for transfer (Step 1b, Section 1.3) are implemented in a specified target setting. In other words, it helps ensure that the protocols and standards defined in the intervention are effectively applied in practice.

Beyond increasing the chances that new interventions achieve their desired outcomes, implementation is important for at least two other reasons. First, policy makers need to understand how an intervention was implemented to correctly interpret its effects in terms of outcomes measured. Even if a quantitative evaluation of an intervention shows that it is effective in terms of relevant health outcomes observed, policy makers can only understand causality if they know which components of the planned intervention were actually delivered and how well this was done. Again, an observed failure could result from poor implementation while success could be due to an intervention that, in practice, was very different from what was intended (Durlak and DuPre, 2008[97]). As discussed further below and in the section on preparing implementation and in Step 3 (Evaluate), an evaluation of the intervention should therefore also include implementation-related indicators. Second, an understanding of the process of implementation, and in particular the factors that contributed to success or failure of initial implementation of a new intervention, is necessary to understand whether an intervention has to be adapted further. A problem related to implementation is that interventions, even if successful in an initial test or pilot phase, are often not sustained over time and therefore fail to deliver their potential in the longer term (ibid.).

2.1.2. Conceptual approach to implementation

For the reasons discussed above, the importance of implementation cannot be overstated. At the same time, policy makers who decide that an intervention should be transferred to a target setting and who allocate funding are rarely the same people who deliver an intervention to the targeted population. Rather, policy makers usually rely on existing health and social care organisations and their staff to deliver the intervention. The ultimate effects of interventions usually depend on changes in behaviours of the citizens or patients the intervention tries to reach. There are thus many intermediary steps between policy that aims to achieve a specified outcome through selecting and funding interventions and the ultimate achievement of these outcomes, which require the concerted effort of many different people. Research on diffusion and implementation of innovations clearly shows that, even if new interventions prove effective and make intuitive sense, they are not implemented spontaneously or naturally (Brownson et al., 2015[99]; Jenkins, 2003[96]). Indeed, implementation may be the greatest challenge in successfully transferring an intervention from one setting to another.

All of this highlights the need for formal implementation processes.[5] Theory and findings from implementation research can help with defining formal processes. There is a growing literature that provides a range of theories, models and frameworks that can underpin the implementation of health-related interventions in general as well as specific types of interventions (see, for example, Brownson et al. (2015[99]) and Nilsen (2015[98])). This literature sometimes suggests that using theoretical approaches will help reduce the gap between evidence and practice that is often deployed (Nilsen, 2015[98]). At the same time, critics have argued that theory is not necessarily better than common sense for guiding implementation (ibid.). It may therefore make sense to focus on a small set of key considerations in implementation without unnecessarily over-complicating the effort.

To increase the chances that an intervention achieves its desired outcomes through successful implementation, policy makers should focus on ensuring that an implementation plan exists, that it lays out the main tasks and responsibilities of people involved, and that it specifies when their tasks will be performed. This section thus conceptualises implementation in terms of "who does what, when".

For understanding the roles of people involved in implementation and defining their specific responsibilities and tasks, implementation can be thought of as the interaction of three systems, as suggested by Wandersman et al. (2008[100]): 1. the synthesis and translation system; 2. the delivery system; and, 3. the support system. The term *system* refers to a set of coherently organised tasks carried out by specific people. The primary tasks of each system and the types of professionals that constitute each system are outlined in Table 2.1. For implementation to be successful, the three systems need to work together.

Table 2.1. Three interacting "systems" in implementation

Based on the interactive systems framework for dissemination and implementation

System	Primary tasks	People responsible for tasks
1. Synthesis and translation	<ul><li>Distil information from research and translate it into a user-friendly format for implementation in the field, for example through preparing manuals;</li><li>Plan implementation and documenting the implementation protocol;</li><li>Allocate resources to the delivery system and support system and ensuring that capacity is available;</li><li>Design evaluation of implementation</li></ul>	**Planners** including:<ul><li>Policy makers;</li><li>Public health specialists;</li><li>Health service and operations researchers</li></ul>
2. Delivery	<ul><li>Carry out the activities that are part of the intervention;</li><li>Adapt the intervention while implementation is underway while remaining faithful to the core components of the intervention (implementation fidelity);</li><li>Interact with citizens/patients who participate in the intervention</li></ul>	**Implementers**, or *frontline* staff, including:<ul><li>Health and social care professionals;</li><li>Public health specialists</li></ul>
3. Support	<ul><li>Provide training prior to implementation, for example through providing general training/coaching to enhance skills and motivation in the delivery system and training specific to the intervention;</li><li>Provide technical assistance while implementation is underway;</li><li>Supervise and monitor implementation, through evaluating fidelity while implementation is underway;</li><li>Evaluate implementation</li></ul>	**Supporters** including:<ul><li>Public health specialists;</li><li>Health service and operations researchers;</li><li>IT specialists;</li><li>Administrative assistants</li></ul>

Note: Some people involved in the implementation of an intervention might be part of several systems at the same time. For example, people who are responsible for the intervention overall, and the teams that support them, might be both, planners and supporters. In particular in small-scale interventions, some people may be planners, implementers and supporters.
Source: Adapted by the authors from Wandersman et al. (2008[100]), "Bridging the gap between prevention research and practice: The interactive systems framework for dissemination and implementation", https://doi.org/10.1007/s10464-008-9174-z.

The implementation of interventions goes through two sequential phases: preparation of the implementation and the actual implementation itself. A core set of steps need to be completed in each of these phases (see Figure 2.1). The preparation phase of implementation is closely intertwined with, and should directly flow from, the activities in Steps 1a and 1b (Sections 1.2 and 1.3). In this first phase, people who are part of the synthesis and translation system, referred to in this section as *planners*, are at work to select best practice interventions based on available evidence, assess transferability and adapt it to the context of the target setting. The preparation phase also includes activities such as writing an implementation plan, and, crucially, building capacity in the delivery and support systems. Capacity is the availability of the necessary resources so that people in the delivery system, referred to as *implementers*, can deliver the intervention. These implementers are then responsible for delivering the intervention as planned, while people in the support system, the *supporters*, provide assistance and monitoring throughout.

A particular challenge in implementation is ensuring that the implementers "stick to the plan" that has been laid out for the intervention while giving them sufficient flexibility to make adaptations. The extent to which delivery of an intervention adheres to the plan during implementation has been frequently referred to as implementation *fidelity* (Carroll et al., 2007[101]; Breitenstein et al., 2010[102]). Fidelity needs to be monitored and evaluated, as discussed below. There can be an inherent tension between implementation fidelity and flexibility. However, there is not necessarily a trade-off between fidelity (i.e. sticking to the original intervention) and adaptation (to better suit the needs of the implementer context) during delivery of an intervention. Box 2.1 discusses how both can be achieved.

> ## Box 2.1. Adaptation of interventions versus fidelity in implementation
>
> While implementation fidelity is central to the effectiveness of an intervention, both, fidelity and adaptation, can contribute to achieving the intended outcomes of interventions (Durlak and DuPre, 2008[97]). Evidence suggests that fidelity does not usually reach 100% and that providers often replicate some parts of an intervention but modify others (Durlak and DuPre, 2008[97]). If implementers are knowledgeable about the communities in which they work and the workflows in their organisations, which is usually the case, they can be expected to be in a good position to make adaptations to an intervention during its delivery that make it more effective in the specific context. At the same time, the intervention must remain faithful to its core components that, based on theory and prior evidence, are expected to make it effective. Fidelity tends to be higher where an intervention fits well with the current mission, priorities, and existing practices at the organisation that delivers the intervention. This suggests that some adaptions are necessary during the delivery of interventions.
>
> The key to successful implementation is **distinguishing between adaptation during delivery that is desirable or necessary**, to make an intervention more effective in unforeseen ways given the specific context, **and undesirable adaptation that could jeopardise the core components of an intervention** likely to make it effective. It is therefore important to specify, ideally during the transferability assessment discussed in Step 1b (Section 1.3) but no later than during the preparation of implementation, the components that constitute the theoretical core of an intervention and monitor how these core components are delivered or altered when the intervention is implemented. Core components should receive emphasis in terms of fidelity while less central components of the intervention can be altered to achieve a good fit with the context and environment. Keeping track of what is altered is also important for evaluating the outcomes of the intervention. Evaluation methods and indicators may need to be adapted to take into account changes of the intervention that occurred during implementation.
>
> Source: Based on Breitenstein (2010[102]), "Implementation fidelity in community-based interventions", https://doi.org/10.1002/nur.20373; Carroll et al. (2007[101]), "A conceptual framework for implementation fidelity", https://doi.org/10.1186/1748-5908-2-40; and Durlak and Pre (2008[97]), "Implementation Matters: A Review of Research on the Influence of Implementation on Program Outcomes and the Factors Affecting Implementation", https://doi.org/10.1007/s10464-008-9165-0.

The remainder of Step 2 – Implement – lays out a set of critical steps that should be covered throughout the two phases of implementation: preparing implementation and implementing. The main steps in each of the two phases are shown in Figure 2.1 and described in detail in the sections that follow.

Figure 2.1. Guidebook overview – Step 2: Implement an intervention

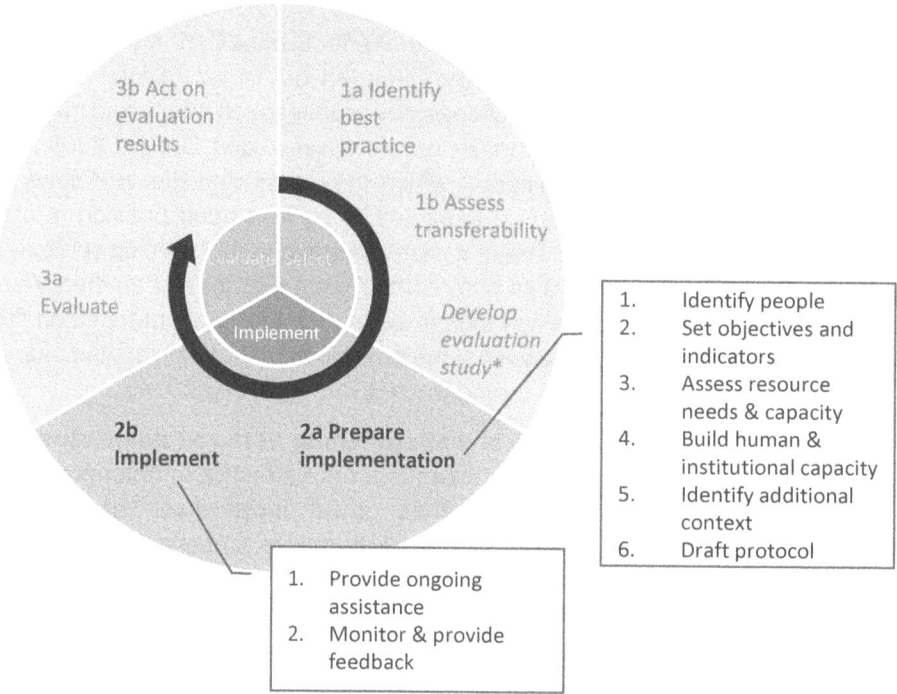

The content of this section is loosely based on the Quality Implementation Framework by Meyers, Durlak and Wandersman (2012[103]), findings from the CHRODIS-PLUS Joint Action (Fullaondo, Txarramendieta and De Manuel, 2018[104]; Palmer et al., 2019[105]; Stegeman et al., 2020[58]) and other findings from the literature. It is also illustrated by practical examples from prior Joint Actions, interventions reviewed by the OECD and the literature. In line with the wider OECD Framework presented in this guidebook, the section is deliberately general, to include a wide range of different public health interventions. References to more specific guidance documents for implementation of certain types of health-related interventions is in Box 2.2.

The two phases of implementation usually occur sequentially in a single implementation of an intervention. However, larger interventions might go through successive iterations of pilot implementations and scaling so that interventions are first implemented on a small scale and evaluated before a larger-scale implementation is prepared.

> **Box 2.2. Other resources to guide the implementation of health interventions**
>
> Various organisations and authors provide resources to guide the implementation of specific types of health-related intervention. A non-exhaustive list of resources that can guide the implementation of health promotion and non-communicable disease interventions includes:
>
> - Manuals by WHO on population-based salt reduction strategies (WHO, 2010[106]), marketing of foods and non-alcoholic beverages to children (WHO, 2010[107]).
> - WHO resources for implementing tobacco control measures (https://www.who.int/tobacco/control/en/), including those developed as part of the Framework Convention on Tobacco Control (https://fctc.who.int/coordination-platform/resources).
> - Guidance resulting from the EU "CHRODIS PLUS" joint action has resulted in a number of guidance documents for the implementation of health-related interventions in general and for more specific types of interventions, including:
>   - Recommendations for the implementation of health promotion good practices (Stegeman et al., 2020[58])
>   - Chronic disease interventions in general (Fullaondo, Txarramendieta and De Manuel, 2018[104])
>   - Interventions that promote physical activity (Barnfield, Savolainen and Lounamaa, 2020[54])
>   - Interventions that manage patients with multi-morbidity (Palmer et al., 2019[105])
>   - The guide for the implementation of CHRODIS PLUS recommendations and criteria to improve the quality of care for people with chronic diseases (WP7 core writing group, 2020[108]).
> - Resources resulting from the EU "JANPA" joint action on prevention of overweight and obesity in children and adolescents (http://janpa-toolbox.eu/).
> - Handbooks for implementation of mental health promotion interventions (Leschied, Saklofske and Flett, 2018[109]; Barry et al., 2019[110]).

2.2. Step 2a: Preparing implementation

Implementation begins with the preparation phase, which, depending on the size and complexity of the intervention, can require significant effort. **Most of the critical steps of implementation occur during this phase**, before actual delivery of the intervention begins (Meyers, Durlak and Wandersman, 2012[103]).

Many activities during preparation, albeit not all, are closely intertwined with the assessment of transferability and adaptation of the intervention to the context of the target stetting, as described in Step 1b, Section 1.3. While assessing transferability is concerned with understanding if the intervention *can be* delivered in the target setting, preparing implementation goes further than that and **aims to ensure that the intervention *is actually* delivered**. To make this happen, a **central objective of the preparation phase is to build implementation capacity**, in terms of human and institutional capacity, and ensuring that the attendant requirements for funding are met. Capacity for implementation is essential for professionals and organisations in the delivery system and their success or failure in implementation depends on all the factors that contribute to capacity (Durlak and DuPre, 2008[97]; Wandersman et al., 2008[100]). **Another objective is to anticipate as many of the risks** that could jeopardise the intervention in the specific target setting and ensure that these are addressed before they materialise.

The **planners** who constitute **the synthesis and translation system take the leading role** in this phase, such as policy makers, public health specialists and health service and operations researchers (see Table 2.1). However, implementers also have to be actively involved to ensure that the intervention can be integrated with existing processes and workflows and to take detailed account of contextual factors that may impact delivery of the intervention, and ultimately its outcomes. Planners may face a number of common challenges during preparation. Box 2.3 lists common challenges in this phase of implementation and possible approaches to meeting them.

Box 2.3. Common challenges in preparation and possible strategies to meet them

Planners are likely to encounter at least some of the following, common challenges when preparing implementation.

Challenge	Possible approaches to meeting this challenge
Stakeholder resistance	Engage stakeholders, including civil society
	Adopt a public communications strategy, including engagement of the media
	Create alliances with stakeholders who are supportive of the intervention
	Gain support from local leadership, including policy makers and managers
	Embed the intervention in organisations whose missions goals are aligned
	Initially focus implementation on people (providers and participants) who are open to change and motivated to create "early success stories" that build support
	Identify and foster local champions who can catalyse enthusiasm and acceptance of the intervention in existing structures
Lack of political support	Ensure intervention aligns with overarching political priorities (see Section 1.3.2, "Political context")
	Ensure close collaboration and/or contact with key political leaders throughout the implementation period, including updates on progress and outcomes (if available)
	Identify a "champion" within the political sphere to provide ongoing support
Lack of understanding of intervention by implementers or lack of skill	Document the core components of the intervention concisely and define the scope for adaptation
	Document the general skills implementers are required to have and align staffing plans
	Organise in-depth training for all implementers to gain intervention-specific knowledge and skills
	Allow implementers to visit sites that have already implemented the intervention previously, to understand characteristics of the intervention and the context of prior implementations
Lack of capacity in organisations expected to implement the intervention	Prepare detailed descriptions of resources needed and tasks to be performed to implement the intervention
	Compare resource needs to existing capacity and identify and fill gaps
	Build active support by senior leaders of implementing organisations so that staff perceive the implementation as conducive to their career rather than an additional burden or career risk
Staffing shortages	Adapt intervention to make better use of existing staff
	Hire additional staff
Funding gaps	Adapt intervention to make better use of existing structures and resources
	Reduce the scope of the intervention to make it feasible with existing funding constraints
	Engage stakeholders to gain further political support and raise additional funds

Source: Based on Barnfield, Savolainen and Lounamaa (2020[54]), "Health Promotion Interventions: Lessons from the Transfer of Good Practices in CHRODIS-PLUS", https://doi.org/10.3390/ijerph17041281; and Jenkins (2003[96]), "Building a better health: A handbook of behavioural change", https://www.paho.org/hq/dmdocuments/2010/9275115907_reduce.pdf.

Preparing implementation comprises at least six key steps, which are shown in Figure 2.1 and described in detail below. These steps are presented in a logical sequence. However, they do not necessarily occur sequentially and in this order. In practice, many of the tasks might be performed in parallel. They are also interrelated. Several iterations of the various steps might be necessary, for instance to reassign roles and responsibilities, to re-train staff or make other adjustments as new contextual information becomes available, until preparation is completed and a final implementation protocol can be written. In some cases, for instance for small and straightforward interventions or when sufficient implementation capacity is already available, certain steps might be skipped.

For many interventions, **one output of the preparation phase is an implementation protocol or plan** – in other words, comprehensive documentation of the remaining implementation process. The main components of an implementation protocol are spelled out in more detail below. Of course, the need for formality in implementation and the extent of such documentation increases with the size of the intervention and the number of stakeholders involved. The implementation of a small-scale intervention that targets no more than a few dozen people and is delivered by a small group of professionals that are close to the organisation that selected and funds the intervention requires less formality and less documentation than a large-scale intervention that is delivered to hundreds or thousands of people by a broad group of professionals and involves many stakeholders. Policy makers need to make good judgment of the level of formality required.

2.2.1. Identifying people who actively contribute to implementation and all other stakeholders

The preparation phase of implementation begins with **identifying all people involved in implementation and mapping out their roles**. This is a task for the planners, most likely the people or organisation who selected the intervention and decided that it should be transferred in the target setting, such as a regional government or health authority, or local health care provider network. In this step, people in the synthesis and translation system also define which organisations and individual people who make up the delivery and support systems.

Agreement should be reached on **which entity takes on organisational responsibility** for delivery of the intervention. Results of the assessment of the political and economic context described in Step 1b (Section 1.3) can guide the identification of the right entity, if this hasn't happened already. The entity can be the same that selected the intervention or a related entity that has a more operational role in the delivery of services related to the public health threat targeted by the intervention, such as a municipal public health department. However, care should be taken that the overall objectives of the intervention are aligned with the mission of the entity that takes on organisational responsibility so that implementation of the intervention is conducive to the achievement of the broader aims of this entity. Committed leadership is a significant enabler of successful implementation (Stegeman et al., 2020[58]).

Roles and responsibilities should be specified in this step for all people who directly contribute to implementation of the intervention. This includes all *frontline* professionals who deliver the intervention through interaction with the target population – the implementers – and all people who assist and support them – the supporters. See Box 2.4 for an example case study.

> Box 2.4. Case study: CHRODIS-PLUS Integrated Multimorbidity Care Model (Aragón, Spain) and Care Integration Pilot (Novo mesto, Slovenia) – roles and responsibilities and stakeholder engagement in implementation
>
> The Department of Health of the Regional Government of Aragón took organisational responsibility for the pilot implementation of the CHRODIS-PLUS Integrated Multimorbidity Care Model (IMCM) across 13 primary care health centres and 3 general hospitals in the region. To ensure that all people who directly contributed to implementation of the intervention were represented in preparation of the implementation, a local implementation working group (LIWG) was formed under leadership of the Department of Health. This group comprised 36 participants from different areas and institutions, including patient representatives, subject matter experts from within and outside of Aragón, and *frontline*

> staff from the primary care centres and hospitals delivering the intervention. The group collectively developed an online educational tool for health professionals participating in the intervention. Eleven members from within the group took on the responsibility for co-ordinating implementation of the intervention following the agreed plan.
>
> In the Novo mesto pilot to integrate care between the hospitals and community health centres, the Novo mesto General Hospital took organisational responsibility for implementation and established a LIWG that included representatives of nearly all stakeholder groups including: hospitals; community health centres; and patient representatives. Representatives from the institutions of various backgrounds joined the LIWG, including surgeons and other physicians, community and hospital nurses, social workers and administrative staff. The involvement of patient representatives in the LIWG was found helpful in finding a "common ground" and basis for communication between the various professional groups involved and ensuring that care integration was approached from the perspective of patient needs. The National Institute of Public Health, representatives of the municipality, health insurance funds and other patient organisations were identified as external stakeholders. They were engaged and encouraged to support the intervention through regular progress meetings and the organisation of community events to discuss patient experiences and barriers encountered.
>
> Source: Gimeno Miguel et al. (2020[111]), "WP6: Pilot implementation of the CHRODIS IMCM in Aragón for improving care of patients with multimorbidity Implementation Report", http://chrodis.eu/wp-content/uploads/2021/01/chrodis-plus-d6.1-pilot-implementation-of-integrated-care-model-for-multimorbidity-1.pdf; Piletič et al. (2020[112]), "WP7- Slovenia Individual pilot action report", http://chrodis.eu/wp-content/uploads/2020/07/a-final-t7.2-slovenia.docx; and personal communications with implementers.

In addition to identifying the organisations and people who are responsible for the intervention and actively contribute to its implementation, **it is helpful to identify and map all other stakeholders** – i.e. people who have an interest in or are affected by the intervention, even if they do not play an active role in the implementation. A particular focus in this process lies with people and organisations who, despite not contributing actively to the implementation, **are in a position to affect implementation of the intervention and its outcomes** This starts in the transferability assessment discussed in Step 1b (Section 1.3), in which the "decision problem" is defined and the "political context" is assessed to gain commitment to and support of the intervention by key decision-makers, such as senior representatives of local authorities.

In this phase of implementation, however, stakeholder mapping needs to be broader and go beyond identifying the main decision-makers whose support is necessary for the intervention to succeed. Other stakeholders obviously include the target population, i.e. the patients or citizens who participate in the intervention and will be served and directly affected by it. But they can also include other government departments, local and regional authorities; industry; associations of health professionals; local universities and research institutes; the media; and NGOs, consumer groups, and other civil society groups that may be active in the field.[6] Again, the need to formally identify, engage and manage stakeholders varies with the size of the intervention and the number of stakeholders involved.

Stakeholder mapping serves two main purposes. First, it helps to identify and engage with all people and organisations who can give relevant input to the implementation of the intervention. This is not only a way to adapt the intervention to the target setting but also a way of creating a sense of ownership among stakeholders, increasing the chances that implementation will succeed. Second, it helps identify all people and organisations whose interests should be taken into account in the implementation and provides a basis for managing them. The OECD provides principles and best practices for governments in consulting stakeholders, to ensure transparency and a balanced representation of interests.[7] These principles can also be applied when engaging stakeholders in public health interventions. A common way of mapping stakeholders for managing them is to identify their respective interests in the intervention and their power to influence it (Ackermann and Eden, 2011[113]). This helps focusing attention on the most important actors:

- Stakeholders with a high level of power and interest require the highest level of attention. Their objectives might be aligned with those of the intervention, in which case they can be harnessed as enablers, or opposed to the objectives of the intervention, in which case they need to be engaged and managed as resistors (also see Griffiths, Maggs and George (2008[114])).
- People with low interest but high power can also be a focus of engagement, to build their awareness and support, converting them to enablers.

Various levers are available for interventions to change behaviours of stakeholders that can ultimately result in health gains. The main levers are discussed in Box 2.5.

Box 2.5. Considering the levers for changing the behaviour of stakeholders

Stakeholder engagement

Engagement of the people who will be affected by an intervention early in its conception and in implementation can, in and of itself, be a strong lever for changing behaviours and, ultimately, achieving the desired outcomes of the intervention. This is because engagement and the opportunity for people to influence and take ownership of the intervention can build self-esteem and intrinsic motivation to participate in its implementation. It also helps adapt the intervention better to the target setting. Stakeholder engagement can help consider cultural norms, openness to new ideas, and the appropriateness of the intervention in the target setting, for instance in terms of economic and social environment. Because health cannot be imposed on anyone, it is important to recognise that interventions are done *with* people rather than *for* the people they aim to reach.

Competition

The desire to emulate and outdo successful peers can be a powerful motivation for changing behaviour. Where ethically sound, this phenomenon can be a harnessed for implementing public health interventions. In particular in large-scale interventions, planners can identify "champions" among the implementers – insiders in the group whose behaviour the intervention aims to change, who are open to change and most motivated to adopt new behaviours or ways of working. Once these people have successfully adopted the core components of the intervention, they can communicate their personal experience. Their anecdotes, enthusiasm and success can push other people to follow. Group insiders have more motivating power than outsiders. Tacit competition, and sometimes envy, among group insiders who share the same problems and culture are stronger motivators than facts and logic.

Provider payment, financial and non-financial incentives

Providing financial and non-financial incentives can facilitate implementation of an intervention. Financial incentives can be considered for people targeted by the intervention and providers delivering the intervention. For providers, non-financial incentives can also be a lever.

To increase uptake in the population or patient target group, interventions should not result in additional financial costs to participants. Direct financial rewards can be offered to people targeted by the intervention and providers delivering it, although this can be costly and may decrease intrinsic motivation. For providers, interventions often result in the shifting of tasks between organisations or individual health professionals. Planners need to understand how such task shifting may affect provider revenues, for example where revenue is generated from fee-for-service (FFS) or case-based payments such as diagnosis-related groups (DRGs), and whether the resulting financial incentives are conducive to or a barrier to successful implementation of the intervention. Changing remuneration schemes for providers can be a strong lever for encouraging implementation.

> In addition to levers such as peer pressure and competition, a range of non-financial incentives can be considered for providers. These include, for example, offering prospects of career advancement, providing tokens of recognition for personal achievement among superiors and peers, reducing workload outside of the intervention and/or offering more flexible working hours, and changes in the organisation that create a more pleasant working environment. Such motivators may be attractive in resource constrained environments, where there is limited funding for financial incentives. However, they have to be designed carefully to be closely aligned with strategic objectives, local cultural and personal norms and values, and circumstances in provider organisations. Putting them in place effectively can therefore require a significant investment of time and energy and commitment among leadership of the organisations involved in the intervention.
>
> **Regulation**
>
> Direct regulation is one way of changing the behaviour of stakeholders that affects the outcome of an intervention. Regulation can, for example, govern the roles and responsibilities of providers who deliver an intervention, restrict the sale, use or consumption of products that are harmful to health and steer health behaviour in a population by promoting healthy and discouraging unhealthy activities. However, regulation may only be appropriate for population-based interventions, in which rules can be applied uniformly to an entire jurisdiction. Effective regulation that achieves its desired effects and avoids unintended consequences can also be difficult to design, time consuming to adopt, and costly to enforce.
>
> Source: Based on International Council of Nurses (2008[115]), "Guidelines: Incentives for health professionals", http://www.whpa.org/sites/default/files/2018-11/WHPA-positive_practice_environments-guidelines-EN.pdf; Jenkins (2003[96]), "Building a better health: A handbook of behavioral change", https://www.paho.org/hq/dmdocuments/2010/9275115907_reduce.pdf; and Promberger (2013[116]), "When do financial incentives reduce intrinsic motivation? Comparing behaviors studied in psychological and economic literatures", https://doi.org/10.1037/a0032727.

2.2.2. Setting measurable objectives and selecting relevant implementation indicators

At this stage, the planners also **set appropriate objectives for implementation of the intervention in the target setting and define relevant indicators** to measure progress towards and achievement of these objectives. This stage can also help understand to what extent the objectives of the intervention are aligned with the existing mission, strategy and priorities of the implementers and the organisations that make up the delivery system. Changes to the composition of the delivery system can be made if it turns out that there are significant conflicts between the objectives of the intervention and the organisational goals of the implementers.

The setting of objectives and indicators for implementation is not a stand-alone exercise. Rather, it should be done as part of designing the evaluation of the intervention and creating the logic model for evaluation, and should ideally occur before implementation (see end of Step 1 (Select) and in more detail in Step 3 (Evaluate), Section 3.2.1). Setting meaningful objectives and indicators has to take into account results of the transferability assessment in Step 1b (Section 1.3) and nearly all other decisions made in the preparation phase. While it should start early, several iterations might be necessary to complete a final version of objectives only towards the end of this phase.

Indicators for implementation are usually related to inputs and activities (see Step 3 (Evaluate), Section 3.2.2) – that is, they are part of the process evaluation that measures if the inputs and activities that make up the intervention have been deployed and delivered as planned. They can also be related to **outputs and intermediate outcomes** – measuring if the delivery of the intervention led to the achievement of intermediary results of the intervention. Frequently used examples of indicators to monitor and evaluate implementation are related to acceptability, adoption (also referred to as uptake), fidelity and cost (Peters et al., 2014[117]; Proctor et al., 2011[118]). Implementation-related indicators are usually not concerned with final outcomes, which are subject of the outcome evaluation that may occur some time after implementation is completed as detailed in Step 3 (Evaluate). See Box 2.6 for example case study related to indicators to measure implementation.

> **Box 2.6. Case study: CHRODIS-PLUS Multimorbidity Care model – implementation-related indicators**
>
> The preparation of implementation of the Integrated Multimorbidity Care Model at the five CHRODIS-PLUS pilot sites, for example, included an explicit step in which planners agreed on key performance indicators (KPIs) for the implementation. Activity-related indicators to monitor implementation of the interventions included, among many others, the existence of a document describing the functions/role of the case manager; the percentage of patients in the intervention for whom a case manager was identified; and, over a specified period of time, the number of visits by complex chronic patients with individual care plans to primary health care centres and the number of health care professional team meetings related to individual care plans.
>
> Source: Palmer et al. (2019[105]), "A Methodological Approach for Implementing an Integrated Multimorbidity Care Model: Results from the Pre-Implementation Stage of Joint Action CHRODIS-PLUS", https://doi.org/10.3390/ijerph16245044.

When defining implementation-related indicators, it is important to keep in mind these **indicators serve two distinct purposes** (Saunders, Evans and Joshi, 2005[119]; Durlak and DuPre, 2008[97]):

1. To **monitor implementation while it is underway**, to provide feedback and make adjustments as necessary. This allows for correcting issues as implementation unfolds to increase the chances that the current implementation in the target setting achieves its objectives.
2. To **evaluate implementation after it has been completed**. This aims to distil and document lessons learnt so that they can be applied in future implementations. These lessons can contribute to improving the same intervention for further transfers to new target settings and future implementations but can also inform implementations of other interventions. Because of the powerful impact of implementation on outcomes discussed above, an assessment of implementation is an integral part of evaluating the intervention and allows for understanding why an intervention may have succeeded or failed.

Consideration therefore needs to be given to **the points in time at which implementation-related indicators are relevant** and whether it is **feasible to generate them at those points in time**. Some indicators are generally relevant during implementation, to monitor, provide feedback and adjust implementation as necessary. Indicators related to inputs and activities, such as the number of trained staff available, the volume of services delivered to participants in the intervention, may typically be relevant for monitoring implementation while it is underway, for example, using administrative data or observing how the intervention is delivered. Indicators that gauge short-term outcomes, such as acceptability of the intervention, might rely on surveys with professionals and patients or citizens. However, it might not always be feasible to conduct these surveys and analyse their results while implementation is underway, either because of time and/or resource constraints or because even short-term outcomes only become apparent after the implementation is completed. This may be an inherent limitation of the implementation process that cannot always be overcome. Nevertheless, planners and supporters can try to rely on informal feedback gathered from implementers of and participants in the intervention, for example through site visits and progress meetings, to gain a sense of how the intervention fares during implementation against indicators of short-term outcomes. See Box 2.7 for an example case study where implementation indicators were monitored during the implementation process.

> **Box 2.7. Case study: Collaborative self-management intervention promoting physical activity (Catalonia, Spain) – implementation-related indicators**
>
> In the implementation of a collaborative self-management intervention to promote physical activity in Catalonia, the planners at Hospital Clínic de Barcelona and the University of Barcelona are defining key performance indicators to be tracked during the first year of implementation. The indicators span inputs, in particular costs of the intervention to the health care system; activities that are part of the intervention, such as the number of participants enrolled compared to the number of participants targeted, and the use by participants of the personal health folder, an electronic tool that provides educational information, self-assessment questionnaires, and apps to monitor physical activity plans; and short-term outcomes of the intervention, including participant satisfaction, emergency department and general practitioner visits, and avoidable hospitalisations and hospital readmissions. KPIs are monitored during implementation. They are also analysed at the end of the first year of implementation to adjust and refine the intervention, and scale it up for regional deployment in all of Catalonia.
>
> Source: Barberan-Garcia et al. (2018[120]), "Protocol for regional implementation of collaborative self-management services to promote physical activity", https://doi.org/10.1186/s12913-018-3363-8; and Barberan-Garcia and Cano (2020[121]), "Assessment of the Prehabilitation Unit at Hospital Clinic of Barcelona: period 2017-2019. NEXTCARE Implementation Report".

2.2.3. Assessing resource needs against existing capacity and readiness

Once the people who will be the implementers and the supporters are identified, the **resource needs for implementation need to be compared to existing capacity** to assess the level of readiness of the existing delivery system and identify gaps. This comparison can guide capacity building – making sure that the delivery system is staffed appropriately, that professionals who are part of the delivery system have all the required skills and that the infrastructure and technical support are available. The larger the gap identified, the more attention has to be paid and effort made to build the necessary capacity.

The assessment of transferability described in Step 1b (Section 1.3) should already provide a good basis for identifying gaps between resource needs and existing capacity. In particular, assessment of the health workforce and the capital resources available in the sector specific context of the target setting (see Table 1.7) and assessment of the economic context (Table 1.9) of the target setting should address much of what needs to be done in this step.

The aim of this step is to increase the level of detail of the analysis and interact directly with the implementers to gain a complete understanding of resource needs and existing capacity. If not yet available already from the transferability assessment, a detailed "costing" exercise can help capture the resource needs of all individual tasks and processes that make up the intervention, in terms of working time of professionals and needs for physical infrastructure, equipment and technical support. The skills professionals need to deliver the intervention also have to be identified. Comparing detailed resource requirements to existing capacity can guide capacity building.

Being realistic when anticipating resources needed is a key enabler of successful implementation (see Box 2.8). Relatedly, the selection of implementation-related indicators and setting of objectives (see above) have to consider what is realistically achievable with the resources available. Experience indicates that implementations often struggle because resource needs, in particular human resources required for implementing an intervention in a new target setting, are often underestimated and objectives may be too ambitious.

> **Box 2.8. Case study: Anticipating resource needs in transfer of health promotion interventions in the CHRODIS-PLUS Joint Action (JA)**
>
> Evaluation from the CHRODIS-PLUS JA highlights the importance of being realistic when setting objectives and anticipating resource needs. Despite recognising this in the implementation framework, planners and implementers in various interventions, including JOGG ("Young People at a Healthy Weight" in Iceland), ToyBox (Malta), the Multimodal Training Intervention (Lithuania and Spain), and the Care Integration Pilot (Slovenia), reported that the time and resources required to undertake certain steps were underestimated. For example, the time needed to translate documentation and materials for participants was underestimated, there was insufficient space on existing premises and infrastructure for conducting meetings, and implementers reported a lack of support and guidance by planners. The ToyBox intervention relied on teachers to deliver the intervention to school children, who reported not receiving sufficient support from the local health promotion and disease prevention authority to enable them to deliver effective sessions. Teachers were asked to follow an implementation manual but would have benefited from more "hands-on" support by planners. In the Care Integration Pilot in Slovenia, implementers reported that they lacked time to deliver the intervention on top of their daily work. Although key personnel were received some remuneration for additional activities that were part of the implementation, such payments did not fully cover incremental working time, leading to unpaid after hours and weekends.
>
> Source: Piletič et al. (2020[112]), "WP7- Slovenia Individual pilot action report", http://chrodis.eu/wp-content/uploads/2020/07/a-final-t7.2-slovenia.docx; Stegeman et al. (2020[58]), "D5.3 Recommendations for the implementation of health promotion good practices: Building on what works: transferring and implementing good practice to strengthen health promotion and disease prevention in Europe", http://chrodis.eu/wp-content/uploads/2021/01/chrodis-plus-d5.3-recommendations-for-the-implementation-of-health-promotion-good-practices-1.pdf; and personal communications with implementers.

By the end of this stage, **a budget for the implementation should be finalised**. The assessment of resource needs and existing capacity should result in a clear idea of the incremental funding that is necessary for the delivery and support system to deliver the intervention, above and beyond the usual operating budget of the organisations that participate. If budget gaps are identified, additional funds can be raised at this stage or the implementation plan adjusted to make the implementation feasible with the budget that is available.

2.2.4. Building human and institutional capacity

Depending on the assessment of resource needs and existing capacity, **significant effort in the preparation phase might need to be put towards building implementation capacity**. This includes both, human capacity in the delivery system, in terms of time and skills of staff, and institutional capacity, in terms of all resources that support the people who deliver the intervention.

Building human capacity includes **ensuring that sufficient staff are available**, either by hiring new staff or freeing up time of existing staff members of organisations that participate in the intervention, and **training the future implementers and supporters**. Not surprisingly, training of staff is a factor that is strongly associated with successful implementation (Durlak and DuPre, 2008[97]). Staffing decisions should make sure that people have the necessary general and professional skills to deliver the intervention. For example, depending on the intervention, there may be a need for teams of physicians with a particular specialisation, community nurses, allied health professionals and support staff, such as information technology specialists. Intervention-specific training builds upon these existing skills to convey the knowledge and competencies necessary to deliver the intervention. If different professionals who will be implementers and supporters are expected to work in teams during implementation, the teams should be defined in this step and their members trained together. For example, in the implementation of a tele-monitoring intervention in Denmark, training in the use of tele-medicine equipment for all professionals in the intervention led not only to confidence in use of the equipment but also to enhanced collaboration between provider institutions due to the diversity of participants in the training sessions (Rasmussen et al., 2015[122]). Joint training sessions, or implementation planning meetings, that involve all staff that contribute to the implementation are not only key in building human capacity but also help create ownership of the intervention among staff (see Box 2.9).

> **Box 2.9. The importance of creating ownership in building human capacity**
>
> Experience from the transfer of good practice intervention in the CHRODIS-PLUS Joint Action (JA) suggests that it can be difficult to "transfer" complex interventions that aim to change workflows in health and social care. This is because a top-down approach to having staff implement a pre-specified intervention that was developed for another context may result in scepticism and resistance, especially if the intervention is perceived to create incremental workload. Therefore building human capacity in preparing implementation is not only about training but also about creating intrinsic motivation and a sense of ownership of the intervention among key staff, through a recognition among them that there is a shared issue at hand that the intervention will help change. Joint training sessions can allow implementers to discuss the problem at hand and find their own solutions, even if these turn out to be similar to those already foreseen in the intervention.
>
> Source: Personal communications with planners and implementers in interventions of the CHRODIS-PLUS JA.

At the end of training, all staff involved in the implementation should have **a clear and consistent idea of why, when, where, with whom and how to implement what**. They should also be reasonably self-sufficient, individually and as teams where necessary, in performing the tasks that constitute the intervention (Meyers, Durlak and Wandersman, 2012[103]).

Building **institutional capacity is an essential step to establish the support system for implementation**. It includes preparing all infrastructure that will support the implementation and creating an environment that is supportive of and conducive to delivering the intervention as intended. Infrastructure can include physical space, such as meeting or patient consultation rooms, digital information and communication technology (ICT), transportation, and whatever else may be immediately necessary for delivering the intervention. A conducive environment provides support and motivation. For large interventions, this can include the recruitment and training of dedicated staff who do not interact directly with the target population but support the people who deliver the intervention. These people can include public health and health service researchers, IT specialists and administrative staff. For smaller interventions, this type of support may be provided by existing staff of institutions that are involved in the implementation. In both cases, these people need to be trained to understand their role in the intervention and have the necessary time and skills to support implementation. Creating a conducive environment also comprises engagement of people who have no formal role in implementation but are present because they work in the same institution as the implementers, or in the immediate vicinity. This can take the form of informing people that are close to the intervention of its implementation, improving existing communication channels and establishing new links to stakeholders.

2.2.5. Identifying additional contextual factors to plan integration with existing processes and workflows, and define scope for further adaptation

The interaction between implementers, supporters and planners, who oversee implementation and provide intervention-specific training, is an opportunity to **involve implementers in detailed planning of the implementation**. This is an important step of the preparation phase for several reasons.

First, shared decision-making and active participation of the implementers in preparation **can create a sense of ownership**, which can in turn enhance implementation and increase the likelihood of longer-term sustainability (see Box 2.9 and Durlak and DuPre (2008[97])). At the same time, the necessary core components of an intervention should not be altered. The core of the intervention should be well established and documented by this stage. This will allow implementers to understand how flexible they can be in delivering the intervention. If any additional adaptations to the core are suggested at this stage, they need to be analysed in detail to assess whether they are necessary and might increase the likelihood of achieving desired outcomes or whether they might undermine the intervention. Any **adaptations to the core should be documented and integrated** with any adaptations that were made when the intervention was assessed for transferability (Step 1b (Assess transferability), Section 1.3). (The case study in Box 2.10 provides an example of how an intervention can be adapted to suit local cultural needs.)

Second, engagement with all implementers and supporters during preparation allows for **identifying additional contextual factors** that help appreciate how well the intervention can be integrated with existing processes and workflows. Much of this work should have already occurred by the time implementation is being prepared, as described in Step 1b (Section 1.3). But it is possible, and indeed likely, that not all contextual factors have been identified in detail upfront. Many gaps can be identified at this stage.

Third, staff in the delivery and support systems can help complete the mapping of stakeholders and the plans and strategies for engaging them as deemed necessary. This helps **anticipate process dependencies and barriers to implementation**. Barriers can be categorised into those that can be proactively addressed and those that are beyond the immediate control of the people who implement the intervention. Contingency plans can be formulated for the latter.

> **Box 2.10. Case study: StopDia for a minority population (Finland) – adapting an intervention**
>
> StopDia is a lifestyle intervention that aims to prevent type-2 diabetes mellitus (T2DM). A small Somali community in Finland is characterised by high prevalence of T2DM and its risk factors. The intervention was adapted specifically for this Somali minority, by including members of the target group in preparation of the implementation. Translation and cultural adjustments to the intervention were completed by a Somali researcher, who also implemented the intervention through group meetings at a local mosque. The researcher was supported by volunteer students, who were also a part of the Somali community. The University of Eastern Finland, the VTT Technical Research Centre of Finland, and the Finnish Institute for Health and Welfare, who developed the StopDia intervention, provided training to the implementers and ongoing support with digital tools used in the implementation.
>
> Source: Hussein et al. (2020[123]), "Health and wellbeing for all – development and implementation of a culturally sensitive lifestyle intervention for Somalis in Finland through the adoption of JA CHRODIS recommendations and set of criteria"; and Pihlajamäki et al. (2019[124]), "Digitally supported program for type 2 diabetes risk identification and risk reduction in real-world setting: Protocol for the StopDia model and randomized controlled trial", https://doi.org/10.1186/s12889-019-6574-y.

2.2.6. Drafting the implementation protocol

Overall, the stages described above should **result in some form of implementation plan or protocol** that will guide the remaining implementation. An implementation protocol contains at least the key components listed in Table 2.2 and spells each of them out in some detail.

An **implementation manual can be part of the implementation protocol** or be drafted as a separate document that accompanies the protocol. While the implementation protocol guides the entity that has organisational responsibility for the implementation and includes all aspects of implementation, the manual only includes operational guidance that supports delivery of the intervention. It is a hands-on resource for implementers and supporters.

Table 2.2. Key components of the implementation protocol

Protocol component	Main content	Included in implementation manual?
Objectives	Description of the overall objective of the intervention and of the set of measurable objectives related to implementation of the intervention in the target setting	Yes
Intervention core components	Specification of a small set of activities and processes that are integral parts of the intervention and cannot be altered	Yes
Roles & responsibilities	Descriptions of specific tasks and responsibilities of all staff involved in delivering the intervention and monitoring implementation	Yes
Process maps and timelines	Detailed visualisations of relationships between staff, process workflows and related timelines for implementation	Yes
Technical assistance	Descriptions of all assistance available to staff who deliver the intervention, including support with infrastructure and equipment and any other technical assistance that is related to the intervention	Yes
Stakeholder analysis and engagement plan	Map of all stakeholders who have an interest in the intervention or can influence it and strategies to engage them as necessary	Yes, to the extent necessary for staff to understand their roles & responsibilities
Performance indicators and monitoring	Indicators monitored during implementation and description of feedback loops to ensure that indicators are communicated, discussed and acted upon	Yes, to the extent that staff and participants in the intervention have to be informed of the data collected and need information on indicators to act upon them.
Management oversight	Role of the entity that has organisational responsibility for the intervention	Yes, to the extent necessary for staff to understand their roles & responsibilities
Evaluation plan *	Indicators and data sources for final evaluation of implementation after it is completed	Yes, to the extent that staff and participants in the intervention have to be informed of the data collected. Some indicators may not be revealed until after implementation to avoid bias.

Notes: The level of detail needed in the implementation protocol and manual increases with the size and complexity of the intervention and the number of stakeholders involved. * Evaluation of the implementation might be part of the implementation protocol and/or the evaluation framework described in Step 3, Section 3.2.

2.3. Step 2b: Implementing

Following careful preparation, the most difficult part of implementation begins – **ensuring that the intervention is actually delivered as planned**. Much of the success or failure of implementation in this phase depends on how well implementation has been prepared and whether the people who deliver the intervention have the necessary capacity.

The **implementers and supporters take the leading role** in this phase (see Table 2.1). The planners, i.e. policy makers, public health specialists and health service and operations researchers, who make up the synthesis and translation system, take on the less active role of monitoring and providing assistance.

This is not to understate their importance. In addition to assistance provided by the support system, ongoing monitoring as implementation unfolds can be key to success by providing supportive feedback and guiding corrective actions, identifying additional resource needs, and helping ensure that the environment in which the intervention is delivered remains conducive. Planners, implementers and supporters may face a number of common challenges during implementation. Box 2.11 lists common challenges in this phase of implementation and possible approaches to meeting them.

> **Box 2.11. Common challenges during implementation and possible strategies to meet them**
>
> Planners, implementers and supporters are likely to encounter at least some of the following, common challenges when implementing an intervention.
>
> | Challenge | Possible approaches to meeting this challenge |
> | --- | --- |
> | Loss of fidelity to the core components of the intervention | Define core components and scope for adaptation during implementation clearly during the preparation phase
Monitor activity- and output-related indicators that measure implementation fidelity
Provide ongoing support to implementers while implementation is underway to reinforce adherence to the core components |
> | Limited uptake of the intervention in the targeted patient/population group | Involve representatives of the target group during the preparation phase
Elicit personal characteristics of people targeted and pay special attention to people who are less likely to participate
Provide clear and easy to understand information to people target about the goal and benefits of the intervention
Pay attention to practical barriers to participation and organise interactions with target groups in a way that makes it as easy to participate |
> | Insufficient time by providers to deliver the intervention as planned | Shift tasks between professionals and/or provider organisations
Review tasks and remove non-essential activities
Allocate additional staff to the intervention, if possible |
> | Challenges with using technology, in particular novel digital tools that support the intervention | Provide ongoing support and re-training to implementers with the use of technology |
>
> Source: Based on Jenkins (2003[96]), "Building a better health: A handbook of behavioral change", https://www.paho.org/hq/dmdocuments/2010/9275115907_reduce.pdf; and de Waard et al. (2018[125]), "Barriers and facilitators to participation in a health check for cardiometabolic diseases in primary care: A systematic review", https://doi.org/10.1177/2047487318780751.

2.3.1. Monitoring implementation and providing supportive feedback

To ensure that assistance is provided where needed most and that the necessary level of implementation fidelity is achieved, **implementation should also be accompanied by monitoring and supportive feedback loops** (Greenhalgh et al., 2004[126]; Fixsen et al., 2005[127]). This means that it should not only be up to implementers to raise issues and ask for support. Rather, planners or the entity that has organisational responsibility for the implementation should proactively monitor implementation by collecting and analysing data, and feeding information back to people who deliver the intervention. This will help ensure that this information is discussed and acted upon (see Box 2.12 for example case study).

> **Box 2.12. Case study: CHRODIS-PLUS health promotion interventions for children and older adults (Iceland, Lithuania and Spain) – monitoring implementation**
>
> In the implementation of CHRODIS-PLUS pilot interventions, a standard reporting template was developed and regularly filled in by implementers to report progress during implementation. The template asked short and basic questions that allowed project leaders to gain an understanding of the progress that was being made, as well as the practical barriers that implementers faced, and to provide support. Questions included:
>
> - What did you do this month?
> - What was recorded (quantitatively or qualitatively)?
> - What were the successes?
> - Were there any barriers?
> - Was any support needed?
> - What are you planning to do next month?
> - What are the perceived barriers?
> - How certain are you that you will achieve what you are planning to?
>
> Source: Barnfield, Savolainen and Lounamaa (2020[54]) "Health Promotion Interventions: Lessons from the Transfer of Good Practices in CHRODIS-PLUS", https://doi.org/10.3390/ijerph17041281.

Information from the monitoring process should be fed back in a supportive manner, to provide an opportunity for improvement and organisational or personal learning. This can either lead to making corrective actions to ensure that implementation fidelity is achieved or to adaptations of the intervention. Adapting parts of the intervention can also be a necessary response to problems that might arise during this phase. Adaptations should be made in concertation with the synthesis and translation system.

One way of providing supportive feedback to implementers is to disseminate internally any positive results observed when monitoring implementation. Dissemination refers to the active spreading of information to a target audience via determined channels (Tabak et al., 2012[128]; Yuan et al., 2010[129]). As positive results emerge, their **dissemination to all implementers and other stakeholders who are actively involved in the implementation can reinforce motivation, increase fidelity to the core components of the intervention, and foster continued stakeholder support**. This increases the chances that implementation is sustained through its successful completion.

Such reinforcement during implementation is particularly important for large-scale and broad interventions, which may take a long time to implement, are dependent on the co-operation of many implementers and on support by stakeholders. In such interventions, it is helpful to start with "quick wins" – small components of the intervention that are relatively straightforward to implement and that can show visible results quickly. Success stories about quick wins can build a sense of self-efficacy and co-operative skills that help the groups of implementers sustain their efforts in the longer term and equips them for larger successes (Jenkins, 2003[96]).

Informal channels of communication, such as accounts of experience by implementers at meetings and exchange of staff between participating organisations, can be used. As discussed above, "champions" can be identified among implementers to disseminate results (see Box 2.3 and Box 2.5). At the same time, planners and supporters can document intermediate results and use more formal communication channels to disseminate positive results.

As more information on facilitators of and barriers to implementation of the intervention and evidence of its effectiveness emerge during the evaluation of the intervention, dissemination should also target external stakeholders. This is discussed in Step 3, Section 3.4.2.

2.3.2. Providing ongoing assistance

As implementation of the planned implementation unfolds, **assistance has to be provided to the people who deliver the intervention** (see Box 2.13 for example case study). Assistance while implementation is underway is one factor that is strongly related with success (Durlak and DuPre, 2008[97]). Assistance has a broad meaning here – it can include not only practical assistance with equipment, information technology and administrative processes but also any assistance related to the core components of the intervention and their delivery.

Professionals who deliver the intervention may need to **ask questions about the intervention** and the practical problems they encounter. They may also need **a forum for discussion and peer support** as unforeseen contextual factors arise. More resources than planned might turn out to be necessary to perform additional activities, tasks might have to be rescheduled, and parts of the intervention might become redundant. Assistance ensures that professionals who deliver the intervention can handle these problems.

> **Box 2.13. Case study: CHRODIS-PLUS health promotion interventions for children and adults (Iceland, Lithuania and Spain) – support during implementation**
>
> During the implementation of CHRODIS-PLUS pilot interventions, the project leaders of each intervention, backed by teams of external experts and researchers, supported the implementers throughout the implementations. Project leaders made site visits, organised bi-monthly meetings via video-conference and were available for consultation by e-mail and social media channels. Implementers were provided with tools to complete the steps defined in the implementation protocol and were involved in group discussions. Documents from these interactions, including meeting notes, recorded video-conferences and other documentation from the communication were stored and analysed to understand facilitators and barriers in the implementation process.
>
> Source: Barnfield, Savolainen and Lounamaa (2020[54]), "Health Promotion Interventions: Lessons from the Transfer of Good Practices in CHRODIS-PLUS", https://doi.org/10.3390/ijerph17041281.

Re-training and **activities that reinforce concepts and the skills built during training** in the preparation phase are a crucial element of assistance during implementation. As professionals enter a routine, the salience of some of the concepts conveyed during training in the preparation phase might wane. Early monitoring of the implementation combined with retraining increases implementation fidelity (Durlak and DuPre, 2008[97]).

2.4. Conclusion of Step 2

Step 2 of the guidebook provides a general framework for understanding implementation in terms of "who does what, when" and is designed to provide policy makers, who may be far from the *"frontline"* of the delivery of an intervention that has been selected for transfer to a target setting, a practical guide to implementation. The importance of implementation cannot be overstated. As experience clearly shows, even appropriate and well-designed interventions can fail if it they are poorly implemented. Although perhaps less common, intended outcomes can conversely be due to the delivery of an intervention that, in practice, was very different from the one selected for transfer. This calls for a formal process of implementation that ensures that an intervention is delivered as planned – a concept frequently referred to as "implementation fidelity". A clear understanding of how an intervention was implemented is also key to interpreting the results of its evaluation and acting on these results accordingly.

This step of the guidebook breaks down implementation into two sequential phases. First, an extensive phase in which implementation is prepared flows directly from the transferability assessment described in Step 1 (Select). This phase involves identifying people who actively contribute to implementation and all other stakeholders; setting measurable objectives and selecting relevant implementation indicators; assessing resource needs against existing capacity and readiness; building human and institutional capacity; identifying additional contextual factors to plan integration with existing processes and workflows, and defining the scope for further adaptation; and drafting the implementation protocol. Second, the intervention has to actually be delivered to its target group. During this phase in which implementation unfolds, this step of the guidebook suggests ways to increase the likelihood of success by monitoring implementation and providing ongoing assistance to the implementers.

Despite the importance of implementation, policy makers need to assess the level of formality required to implement an intervention, and adapt the process accordingly. The need for formal processes increases with the size of the intervention and the number of stakeholders involved. The implementation of a small-scale intervention, which is delivered by a small group of professionals that are close to the organisation that selected and funds the intervention, may require less formality than one delivered to hundreds or thousands of people by a broad group of professionals and involving many stakeholders. The general principles provided in this step of the guidebook should therefore be applied flexibly and with some common sense, taking into account the type of intervention being implemented. Policy makers can also find guidance for implementation of specific types of intervention in a number of resources listed above.

Step 3. Evaluate

3.1. Introduction to evaluating an intervention

The last step within OECD's guidebook is to evaluate the best practice intervention identified in Step 1 and implemented in Step 2. The structure of evaluating the best practice intervention is broken into two key components: designing and executing an evaluation study (Figure 3.1).

As outlined in Step 1, designing the evaluation study occurs in the early phase of the Plan-Do-Study-Act cycle, specifically, once an intervention has been classified as best practice and appropriate for transfer. Despite this, designing the evaluation study is discussed in Step 3 to cater to those who are solely interested in the evaluation component of the guidebook.

Evaluations are a necessary final step as they provide policy makers with insight into how the intervention is operating and whether or not it achieved (or is on the path to achieving) desired outcomes. Further details on the importance of evaluation are explored in Box 3.1.

It is important to determine at the outset of Step 3 whether people involved in the evaluation have the necessary technical skills. If not, it is possible to partner with an external organisation, such as a research organisation.

Step 3 of the guidebook is applicable to an individual evaluation as well as system-wide evaluations. System-wide evaluations incorporate a wider range of stakeholders from different sectors who undertake activities to meet high-level goals (e.g. United Nations Sustainable Development Goals). These types of evaluations, although more complex, are important for improving overall population health.

Figure 3.1. Guidebook overview – Step 3: Evaluate an intervention

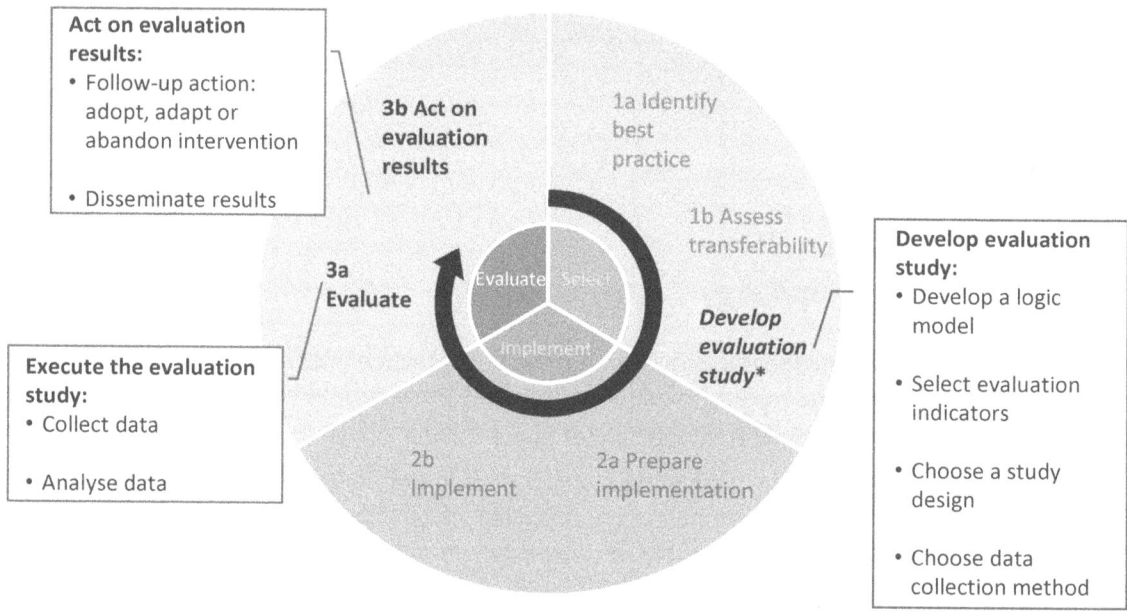

Box 3.1. Why evaluate?

There are various reasons evaluations are not included a project plan, including (O'Connor-Fleming et al., 2006[130]; Lobo, Petrich and Burns, 2014[131]):

- Lack of expertise, time or resources
- Lack of recognition of the benefits of evaluation, especially in the presence of competing priorities (such as service delivery)
- The politics of evaluation, including the potential risk of unfavourable findings
- A "blind" belief in the success of the intervention.

Nevertheless, there are many more reasons that support a rigorous intervention evaluation. In particular, evaluation of a new implemented intervention is crucial to understand whether it is successful – and whether it should be continued or amended. Moreover, evidence from a robust evaluation can provide support for continued investment or expansion of the intervention. Other reasons supporting the incorporation of an evaluation in the project plan from the beginning include:

- To determine the best way to design, deliver and improve the intervention
- To ensure the optimal use of time and resources
- To justify continued funding
- To ensure services are equitable and accessible
- To satisfy questions of accountability, or to fulfil grant or contract requirements
- To advance health promotion by sharing knowledge about effective interventions.

Source: O'Connor-Fleming et al. (2006[130]), "A framework for evaluating health promotion programs", https://doi.org/10.1071/he06061; Lobo, Petrich and Burns (2014[131]), "Supporting health promotion practitioners to undertake evaluation for programme development", https://doi.org/10.1186/1471-2458-14-1315; Public Health Ontario (2016[132]), "Evaluating health promotion programs: introductory workbook", https://www.publichealthontario.ca/-/media/documents/E/2016/evaluating-hp-programs-workbook.pdf?la=en.

3.2. Develop the evaluation study

The first component of Step 3 – Evaluation – is to develop the evaluation study. This involves developing a logic model, selecting evaluation indicators, and choosing a study design and data collection method.

It is not plausible to rigorously evaluate all public health interventions. Therefore an evaluation study should reflect the intervention's size, significance and risk as discussed in Box 3.2.

> **Box 3.2. Prioritising evaluation resources**
>
> In countries such as Australia, governments offer guidance on how to prioritise evaluation efforts. Example criteria policy makers could consider when prioritising evaluation resources are summarised below:
>
> - **Priority**: the overall strategic importance of the intervention in achieving high level objectives as well as the intervention's importance against competing priority areas
> - **Funding**: the overall funding the intervention receives
> - **Risk**: risk associated with the intervention, such as difficulty in assessing intervention outcomes
> - **Impact**: how likely the intervention will affect population health
> - **Evidence**: the existing evidence-base for the intervention to date.
>
> Source: Information provided by the Australian delegation to the OECD Health Committee.

3.2.1. Develop a logic model

The first step in the evaluation process is to develop a logic model (The Better Care Fund, 2015[133]). To evaluate an intervention, there needs to be a clear definition of the intervention's objectives. Generally, this would be an impact on population health, for example, reduction in the prevalence of obesity or the incidence of heart attacks (also referred to as "final outcomes"). It is also important to define the population of interest (Public Health Ontario, 2016[132]). A logic model can help to understand how the intervention will achieve the outcome within the population of interest. It defines the inputs needed for the intervention, the activities or processes that are associated with it and intervention's outcomes (see Box 3.3).

> **Box 3.3. Logic models for evaluation**
>
> A logic model (or "programme logic", "programme theory", "causal model", "conceptual map") summarises the main elements of an intervention, and provides a visual overview of how it leads to the desired outcomes (Centers for Disease Control and Prevention, 2016[134]; Public Health Ontario, 2016[132]).
>
> There is no one standard logic model in the literature, rather there are various terms to explain the same or similar concepts. The order of elements within the logic model may differ depending on how elements are defined. For the purpose of this guidebook, four programme logic elements are used:
>
> - **Inputs**: the resources available to implement and deliver activities
> - **Activities**: the essential activities required to produce intervention outputs
> - **Outputs**: measure the products/good/services that result from implementing an intervention and are required to achieve desired outcomes
> - **Outcomes**: describe the impact of the intervention and therefore whether it is achieving (or has achieved) its objectives.

Various templates and examples can be found online, but these should be used as a guideline only and adjusted to fit the intervention. The design and terminology can be changed to suit the local context.

An example programme logic for reducing the prevalence of adolescent smoking by the New South Wales (Australia) Ministry of Health is in Figure 3.2 (Centre for Epidemiology and Evidence, 2017[135]). For other examples, see WHO's logic model for micronutrient interventions in public health or Public Health Ontario's (Canada) logic model for diet related health problems (Public Health Ontario, 2016[136]).

Figure 3.2. Example programme logic for an intervention to reduce adolescent smoking

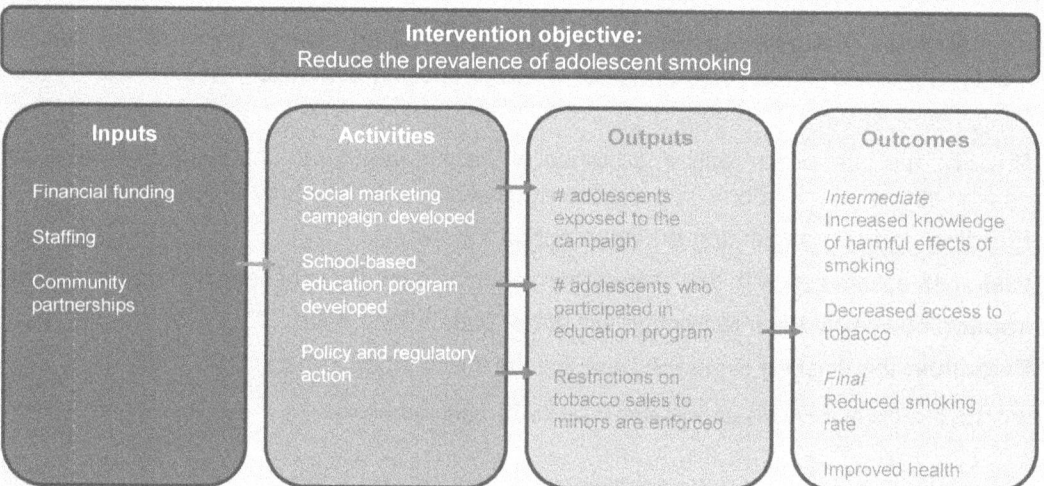

Source: Adapted from the NSW Ministry of Health Centre for Epidemiology and Evidence (2017[135]), "Developing and Using Program Logic: A Guide", https://www.health.nsw.gov.au/research/Publications/developing-program-logic.pdf.

3.2.2. Select evaluation indicators

This section discusses the different types of indicators, how to select high-quality indicators as well as the importance of stratifying data collected from indicators.

Types of indicators

Once the programme logic is developed, indicators for each element within the logic model should be specified (see Table 3.1 for a high-level overview and Figure 3.3 for an example). When choosing indicators, it is important to be realistic by considering the data and resources available.

Inputs: the starting point of an evaluation is the inputs. Input indicators should cover items such as funding (financial resources); personnel required to deliver the intervention (e.g. in FTE); capital infrastructure (e.g. meetings rooms, exercise equipment, community kitchens); other materials and supplies; and in-kind resources. This information is important to put the outcomes in perspective in terms of return on investment of time and money.

Activities: activity indicators reflect the essential activities required to produce intervention outputs (i.e. what to do with intervention inputs). Example activity indicators include training for teachers to deliver obesity prevention curricula; healthy lifestyle workshops for parents and children; and developing advertising material to promote physical activity.

Outputs: output indicators reflect the products/goods/services produced from the intervention's activities. Using the examples provided under "Activities", aligning output indicators include: the number of teachers who received training; the number of healthy lifestyle workshops run; and the number of social media ads promoting physical activity. Output indicators, therefore, help measure how well the intervention was implemented. Without this information, it is possible, for example, to assume erroneously that an intervention has no impact, while in reality the intervention did not actually reach participants.

Outcomes: outcome indicators measure whether the intervention has achieved (or is on the path to achieving) its objectives and align with "effectiveness" indicators used in Step 1a of the guidebook. Outcomes can be broken into two categories – final and intermediate. Final outcomes reflect the ultimate objective of policy makers, and, in the field of public health typically refer to changes in population health (for example, a reduction in the incidence of cardiovascular disease (CVD)). Final outcomes, however, can be difficult to measure and can take many years to achieve. For this reason, intermediate outcomes (often referred to as short- and medium-term outcomes) directly related to the final outcome can be measured. Using CVD prevalence as an example, intermediate outcomes of interest may include a reduction in salt intake and improved knowledge on the importance of a healthy diet. Nevertheless, it is important to carefully consider this causal pathway. For example, a reduced calorie intake will only decrease body-mass index if all else stays equal. In reality physical activity may also decline, which could negate the impact on BMI. In this case, it would be useful to also measure any changes in physical activity.

Generally, indicators at the beginning of the logic model are easier to measure, while indicators at the end of the logic model are more relevant to the health impact of the intervention but more difficult to measure.

Table 3.1. Types of evaluation indicators

Type	Definition
Inputs	Monetary and non-monetary inputs necessary to deliver the intervention (e.g. funding and staffing)
Activities	The essential activities required to produce intervention outputs
Outputs	The products/goods/services produced from the intervention's activities
Outcomes	Whether the intervention is achieving (or has achieved) its objectives. For the purposes of this guidebook, outcome indicators have been broken into two categories: **Intermediate outcomes**: outcomes that are known to relate directly to the final outcome* **Final outcomes**: outcomes of interest to policy makers and in the case of public heath generally refer to tangible changes in population heath (often referred to as long-term outcomes or impacts)

Note: *For the purposes of this guidebook, intermediate outcomes incorporates short- and medium-term outcomes, which is the terminology frequently used in the literature.
Source: CDC (2018[137]), "Program Evaluation Framework Checklist", https://www.cdc.gov/eval/steps/step2/index.htm; Public Health Ontario (2016[132]), "Evaluating health promotion programs: introductory workbook", https://www.publichealthontario.ca/-/media/documents/E/2016/evaluating-hp-programs-workbook.pdf?la=en.

Figure 3.3. Example evaluation indicators across a logic model

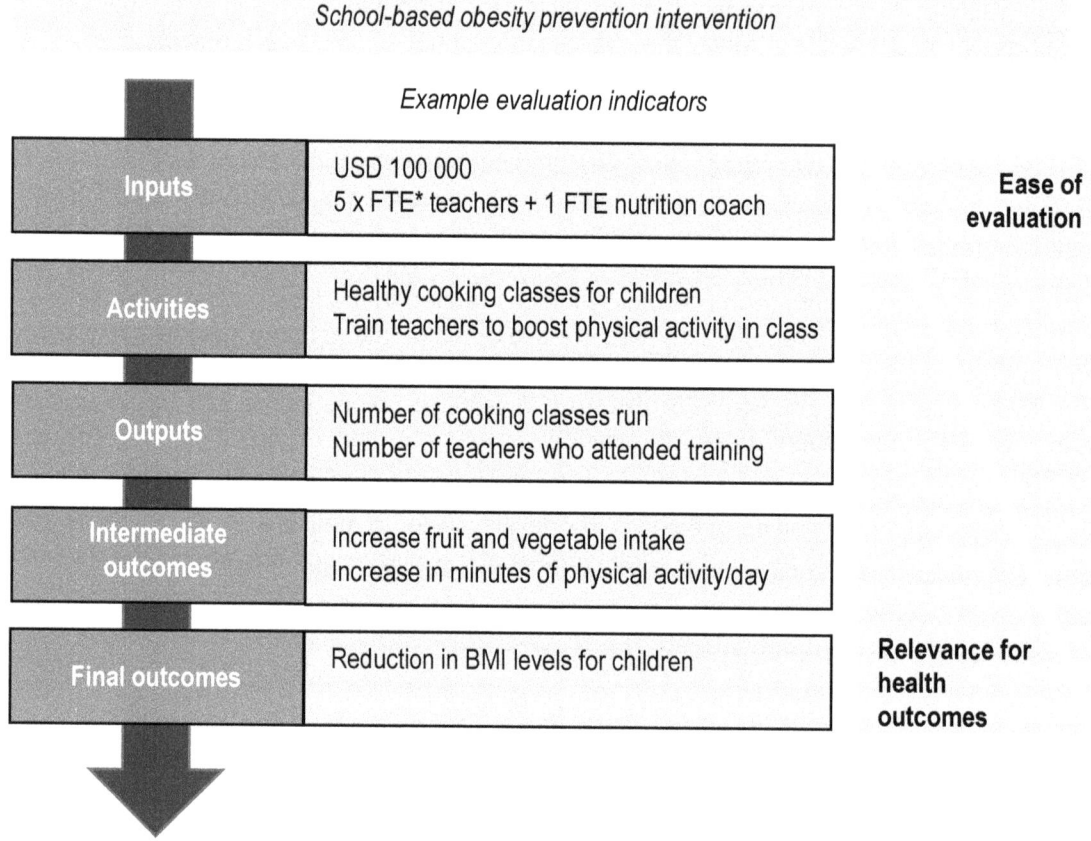

Note: *FTE = full-time equivalent. USD = US dollars. The logic model is a high-level example only, it does not present a logic model previously used to evaluate a school-based obesity prevention intervention.

Useful databases: Outcome indicators

A non-exhaustive list of universally recognised intermediate and final outcome indicators are listed in Annex B. The indicators cover a range of public health issues including risk factors and chronic disease. The Annex also includes links to databases which collect this information, including:

- **OECD Health Statistics**: http://www.oecd.org/els/health-systems/health-data.htm
- **Eurostat**: https://ec.europa.eu/eurostat
- **WHO Global Health Observatory**: https://www.who.int/data/gho/data/indicators
- **Institute for Health Metrics and Evaluation**: http://www.healthdata.org/

Where possible, ancillary outcomes may also be considered, for example the impact of the intervention on the workload of doctors, health care cost or productivity, as well as broader societal considerations such as those outlined within OECD's Better Life Index (see Box 3.4). While not the primary aim of the intervention, these additional benefits can help make the case for investing in the intervention. Similarly, patient experience and well-being can show additional positive impacts of the intervention, or highlight issues with the design.

> **Box 3.4. Measuring well-being as an outcome: The OECD's Better Life Index**
>
> Increasingly governments are moving beyond measures of economic activity to measure societal progress. It has been recognised that progress across a range of sectors is needed to improve people's lives and therefore their well-being. Well-being is important for both the individual and society given its impact on economic growth, productivity, long-term sustainability and societal stability. For example, in 2019, the European Council adopted conclusions from the "The Economy of Well-being" report, which invites member states to put people and their well-being at the centre of policy design. Similarly, in Australia, the Australian Institute for Health and Welfare (the Federal Government's health and welfare statistics agency) has developed a conceptual framework of welfare (and aligned indicators) to assist in evidence-based decision making.
>
> To assist countries in systematically measure societal progress (and therefore well-being), the OECD has developed a well-being framework. The framework consists of 11 key dimensions and aligned indicators (see Table 3.2) (OECD, 2020[138]).
>
> **Table 3.2. OECD Well-being Framework – headline indicators**
>
> | Key dimension | Indicator |
> |---|---|
> | Income and wealth | Household net adjusted disposable income |
> | | Household median net wealth |
> | Housing | Disposable income after housing costs |
> | Work and job quality | Employment rate |
> | Health | Life expectancy at birth |
> | Knowledge and skills | Cognitive skills of 15-year-old students in science |
> | Environmental quality | Access to green space |
> | Subjective well-being | Life satisfaction |
> | Safety | Deaths due to assault |
> | Work-life balance | Time allocated to leisure and personal care |
> | Social connections | Time spent interacting with friends and family as primary activity |
> | Civic engagement | Voter turnout |
>
> Source: OECD (2020[138]), "How's Life? 2020: Measuring Well-being", https://dx.doi.org/10.1787/9870c393-en.
>
> Given the growing interest and importance of measuring well-being, consideration should be given to measuring outcome indicators beyond the health sector. For example, using an intervention to promote physical activity as an example, in addition to changes in BMI, it may be useful to measure the intervention's impact on work-life balance (more time allocated to leisure and personal care) and life satisfaction.
>
> In determining whether to include well-being indicators in an evaluation, **it is important to remember the following**:
>
> - Well-being indicators should not replace intermediate and final outcome indicators, rather they should be complementary to improve evaluation results
> - Additional resources will be needed to collect data for well-being indicators, which may be challenging due to budgetary constraints. Health leadership may consider engaging with other sectors to collect and analyse data of shared interest.
> - Finally, similar to many final outcomes, changes in well-being indicators may take many years to realise and therefore fall outside the evaluation time period.

Choosing high-quality indicators

To assist in the selection of high-quality indicators across the logic model, the following criteria, based on the SMART[8] framework, should be considered (The Better Care Fund, 2015[133]) (Victorian Government Department of Health, 2010[139]):

- **Importance/relevance/utility:** time and resources need to be invested to collect data on any indicator. They should therefore be important and meaningful to evaluate the intervention.
- **Accessibility/feasibility**: data needs to be obtainable, which depends on resource constraints, the availability of the data, and the frequency by which it is made available.
- **Reliability**: indicators should measure the issue or outcome consistently, to allow comparisons over time and between people or groups.
- **Validity/accuracy/robustness**: indicators should accurately measure the concept or event. However, in some cases this is not possible, and proxy measures should be considered (e.g. using income as a proxy for socio-economic status).
- **Timeframe**: it is important to consider the timeframe in which a change in the indicator can reasonably be expected, and whether this falls within the evaluation study period.

Stratifying indicator measures

When studying the impact of public health measures on the population, it is important to look at their effect on inequalities (as discussed in Step 1a – "Equity") (Victorian Government Department of Health, 2010[139]). Inequalities can exist across racial and ethnic groups, regions or neighbourhoods, rural or urban areas, socio-economic groups (see Table 1.2 "Priority population groups" in Step 1a). Pertinent factors for inequalities in the implementation population should be identified, and included in the data collection process (for example, see Step 1 (Select), Table 1.2). This will allow results to be analysed across priority population groups, to see whether the intervention increases or decreases inequalities (e.g. did access and/or outcomes differ across population groups?).

3.2.3. Choose a study design

The two most common forms of evaluation are process and outcome (Centers for Disease Control and Prevention, 2011[140]):

- **Process evaluation**: process evaluations assess whether an intervention was implemented as intended (i.e. implementation fidelity). Process evaluations are therefore interested in examining indicators from the logic model's *input, activities* and *output* elements.
- **Outcome evaluation**: outcome evaluations assess the impact of the intervention on desired outcomes. Outcome evaluations focus on the logic model's *outcome* element, both intermediate and final.

Undertaking both a process and outcome evaluation leads to greater insights. Process evaluations facilitate understanding of the results from an outcome evaluation (i.e. the causes of performance) and therefore provide insight into how an intervention can be improved (Engbers and Sattelmair, 2008[141]). For example, using the case study from Figure 3.3 (school-based obesity prevention), if the outcome evaluation revealed no change in fruit and vegetable intake or a change in BMI, results from the process evaluation can provide insight into why this happened – e.g. what proportion of teachers attended training?

In regard to outcome evaluations, it is important to understand whether changes in outcomes are related to the intervention or external factors occurring simultaneously such as other policies or interventions (i.e. determining causal attribution). Again using the example from Figure 3.3, if the intervention was introduced at a similar time to a ban on junk-food advertisement, a simple examination of outcomes may reflect the impact of the advertisement ban as opposed to the school-based intervention.

The question of causal attribution can be addressed through the study design. There exist different approaches to design an evaluation study (see Box 3.5). A randomised controlled trial (RCT) is the gold standard for measuring the effectiveness of medical interventions in terms of outcomes. However, as discussed in Step 1a, this may not be feasible in a health promotion setting for various reasons: it may not be ethical to withhold the intervention from people; it may be difficult to achieve randomisation in participation; and it may not be possible to avoid "contamination" of the comparison group (O'Connor-Fleming et al., 2006[130]; Sanson-Fisher et al., 2007[142]). A non-randomised controlled trial does not withhold the intervention from willing participants or struggle with randomisation, but still requires access to information on some control group. A pre-post study is often the easiest to achieve, but this requires researchers to pay close attention to potential confounding factors, and may not provide robust evidence.

For the reasons outlined above, it is important to carefully consider which study design is most appropriate. This may involve taking into account factors such as financial resources, available time to evaluate, logistics of collecting data, and the skills/capabilities of those leading the evaluation.

Box 3.5. Study design options for the evaluation of interventions

An evaluation can be carried using one of many study designs. Commonly study designs within the field of public health are listed below. This list is not comprehensive; for further evaluation study designs, see Table 1.3 in Step 1a.

Randomised controlled trial (RCT)

An RCT is the gold standard of study designs. A group of participants is randomly distributed between an intervention and a control group. If the randomisation is done correctly, the two groups will be similar in all respects except for the intervention. As such, any difference between the two groups in outcomes can be ascribed directly to the intervention.

Non-randomised controlled trial

A non-randomised controlled trial compares the outcomes of the participants of the intervention to another group of people who did not participate in the trial. For example, the neighbourhood where the intervention took place could be compared to another neighbourhood where there was no intervention. Alternatively, the control group can be selected from the wider population to match the intervention group (e.g. similar age, gender and baseline measurements). Either way, in this design there remains a risk that the intervention group is inherently different and that this difference somehow contributed to the observed results.

Cluster-randomised trial

This approach could be seen as a mid-way between randomised and non-randomised trials. In a cluster-randomised trial intact social units, such as households, primary care practices, hospital wards, classrooms, neighbourhoods or entire communities, are randomly allocated to an intervention or control arm. While the people in one such unit can be expected to be more similar to each other than if they were distributed individually, there is some degree of randomisation.

> **Pre-post study**
>
> A pre-post study compares the outcomes in the study population before and after the intervention – ascribing a change in the outcome to the intervention. However, this study design cannot account for other elements that may have changed over the time the intervention took place (e.g. seasonality, other interventions or policies).
>
> Source: Thiese (2014[143]), "Observational and interventional study design types; an overview", https://doi.org/10.11613/BM.2014.022; Weijer et al. (2011[144]), "Ethical issues posed by cluster randomized trials in health research", https://doi.org/10.1186/1745-6215-12-100; Clark et al. (2019[145]), "Evaluating the impact of healthcare interventions using routine data", https://doi.org/10.1136/bmj.l2239.

In addition to process and outcome evaluations, policy makers may also be interested in undertaking an economic evaluation. Economic evaluations use results from the outcome evaluation and compare these to input costs (see Box 3.6 for an overview of key cost items). This type of intervention is important given all policy makers face budget constraints. Types of economic evaluations are described in Box 3.7.

> **Box 3.6. Measuring intervention costs for an economic evaluation**
>
> In addition to process and outcome evaluations, policy makers may also be interested in results from an economic evaluation. An economic evaluation assesses costs in relation to benefits to assist policy makers make decisions that maximise outcomes from a limited set of resources.
>
> Intervention costs can be broken into several categories including labour, capital, consumables, administrative and overhead costs (Tan-Torres Edejer et al., 2003[146]). Costs associated with implementing a nutrition and healthy lifestyle in-person intervention, for example, may include:
>
> - The cost of training staff to deliver the intervention (labour)
> - Wages paid to staff responsible for leading physical activity sessions and cooking classes (labour)
> - The cost of renting out gym space to undertake physical activity sessions and kitchen space for cooking classes (capital)
> - The cost of promoting the intervention to eligible participants (e.g. developing promotion material) (administrative)
> - The cost of food used in healthy eating cooking classes (consumables).
>
> When measuring costs it is important to also consider:
>
> - **Discounting**: intervention costs occur at different stages therefore it is important to apply a discount rate to ensure future costs are in a common metric (i.e. their present value). Applying a discount rate means costs incurred today have a higher value than those in the future, which reflects that in general people prefer to receive benefits now but pay for them later. An annual discount rate of around 3% is considered the "norm" in global health amongst developed countries (this figure is higher for less advanced economies) (Haacker, Hallett and Atun, 2019[147]). If costs are discounted, it may also be important to discount outcomes using the same or a different discount rate.
> - **Itemisation**: to the extent possible, costs should be itemised at the unit level. For example, it may be appropriate to assign only a proportion of wage costs to the intervention if wages cover costs to undertake unrelated activities.
>
> Finally, unless considered essential for delivering the intervention, evaluation costs are to be excluded.

> **Box 3.7. Types of economic evaluations**
>
> Economic evaluations assess an intervention's efficiency (see Step 1a, "Efficiency", for further details). Commonly applied economic evaluations in the health sector include cost-utility, cost-benefit, cost-effectiveness analysis. The appropriate economic evaluation depends on how outcomes are measured.
>
> - **Cost-utility analysis (CUA):** CUA provides an estimate of the additional monetary cost of obtaining one QALY (i.e. one year in full health). CUAs are appropriate when assessing multiple public health interventions with different objectives, all of which are converted into QALYs (York Health Economics Consortium, 2016[148]; Sassi, 2006[19]).
> - **Cost-benefit analysis (CBA):** CBA transforms outcome measures into a monetary unit and compares this with the cost of the intervention (i.e. cost-benefit ratio). It provides a net monetary cost of achieving an additional unit of outcome. It is an appropriate technique when outcomes can be translated into monetary terms. CBAs are primarily used when assessing capital projects (such as building a new hospital) (York Health Economics Consortium, 2016[149]), however, they can also be used when measuring the value of a statistical life (i.e. willingness to pay for a reduction in the risk of death). CBAs identify interventions with the largest net benefit, these however, aren't necessarily the most efficient, or the most effective.
> - **Cost-effectiveness analysis (CEA):** CEA calculate estimated costs of an additional outcome unit across one or more interventions. The outcome unit is dependent on the intervention being evaluated (e.g. the cost per extra patient achieving a 10 mm Hg fall in blood pressure) (York Health Economics Consortium, 2016[150]). CEAs are useful when assessing interventions with the same outcome indicator of interest. For example, it is not intuitive to compare the cost of a one-point reduction in BMI with the cost of a reduction in alcohol consumption by one standard drink per week.
>
> Note: In relation to Box 1.4 ("Efficiency indicators") CUA and CBA can be used for universal health-related efficiency indicators, while CEAs can be used for intervention specific efficiency indicators.

3.2.4. Choose a data collection method

Data for the indicators selected can come from a range of sources (see Box 3.8). These include primary datasets (which are collected specifically for the evaluation study) and secondary datasets (which already exist) (The Better Care Fund, 2015[133]). Healthcare systems generate large amounts of data during their routine operations, such as admissions data, registry data, claims data and electronic health record data. Using these routine data sources for an evaluation study requires less investment of time and resources, as the data is already collected. Moreover, data is often available for many years (which can be used to analyse the "before") and for a large population (which can be used to create a control group) (Clarke et al., 2019[145]).

However, routine datasets are per definition not set up specifically to answer the questions of the evaluation study. Primary data collection on the other hand can be fully tailored to the needs of the study. A first step in choosing a data collection method is to identify any routine data sources that could potentially be used. These datasets should be compared to primary data collection in terms of investment needed and suitability of the data.

> **Box 3.8. Potential sources of data**
>
> Data for indicators comes from primary and/or secondary sources. The former involves collecting new information, while the latter relies on previously sourced information. Regarding secondary data, a list of recommended international, publically available datasets is provided in Annex B.
>
> **Primary data**
>
> - Participant data from the intervention (e.g. biomedical measurements, attendance)
> - Process data from the intervention (e.g. records of activities, progress reports, minutes)
> - Surveys (e.g. of participants, providers)
> - Interviews
> - Focus groups
> - Observational data
>
> **Secondary data**
>
> - Population data (e.g. disease registries, census data, mortality data)
> - Healthcare utilisation data (e.g. electronic health records, admissions data, claims data)
> - Document review (e.g. medical records)
> - Routine studies (e.g. provider-run patient experience surveys, national health questionnaires)
>
> Source: Victorian Government Department of Health (2010[139]), "Evaluation framework for health promotion and disease prevention programs", https://www.health.vic.gov.au/publications/evaluation-framework-for-health-promotion-and-disease-prevention-programs; CDC, (2012[151]), "Introduction to Program Evaluation for Public Health Programs: A Self-Study Guide", https://www.cdc.gov/eval/guide/index.htm.

It is recommended to collect both quantitative and qualitative data, to get a full picture of the performance of the programme (The Better Care Fund, 2015[133]; Centers for Disease Control and Prevention, 2012[151]). While quantitative data is often considered reliable and can help draw conclusions about the larger population, qualitative data can provide in-depth information on the functioning of the intervention, by identifying the factors or reasons affecting behaviour or outcomes. Qualitative data can be gathered from open-ended surveys, in-depth interviews, focus groups, narrative and participant observation (Victorian Government Department of Health, 2010[139]).

If primary data is collected, the approach taken needs to be standardised and tested. For interviews, an interview protocol needs to be developed. This can be done following four stages (Castillo-Montoya, 2016[152]):

- Developing interview questions that align with research questions. This also includes omitting any questions that are not necessary, to keep the length of the interview down.
- Constructing an inquiry-based conversation, which asks questions in a way that is understandable to participants, follows a logical conversational flow and may include specific prompts and follow-up questions.
- Receiving feedback on interview protocols (see Box 3.9).
- Piloting the interview protocol. During this try-out, in conditions similar to the real study situation, the interviewer provides feedback on the flow of the interview, any issues with responses and the timing of the interview.

Similar steps can be taken to develop and test survey questions, or a focus group script.

> ### Box 3.9. Check-list for interview protocol review
>
> Collecting information from interviews can be complex. To maximise the quality of objective and subjective information collected as well as ensure high levels of participation, it is important to refine the interview protocol. Drawing upon Castillo-Montoya (2016[152]), the following refinement framework may be used.
>
> **Structure**
>
> - Beginning questions are factual in nature
> - Key questions represent the majority of the questions and are placed between beginning and ending questions
> - Questions at the end of interview protocol are reflective and provide participant an opportunity to share closing comments
> - A brief script throughout the interview protocol provides smooth transitions between topic areas
> - Interviewer closes with expressed gratitude and any intents to stay connected or follow up
> - Overall, interview is organised to promote conversational flow
>
> **Writing of Interview Questions & Statements**
>
> - Questions/statements are free from spelling and grammatical error(s)
> - Only one question is asked at a time
> - Most questions ask participants to describe experiences and feelings
> - Questions are mostly open ended
> - Questions are written in a non-judgmental manner
>
> **Length of Interview Protocol**
>
> - All questions are necessary
> - Questions/statements are concise
>
> **Comprehension**
>
> - Questions/statements are devoid of academic language and jargon
> - Questions/statements are easy to understand
>
> Source: Extract from Castillo-Montoya, (2016[152]), "Preparing for Interview Research: The Interview Protocol Refinement Framework", https://nsuworks.nova.edu/tqr/vol21/iss5/2.

As part of the data collection plan, it is important to determine your study population: the people from whom data will be collected. If the programme is relatively small, it may be possible to include all participants in the evaluation study (Olney and Barnes, 2013[153]; Public Health Ontario, 2016[132]). If this is not possible, the results will rely on a sample. This sample needs to be of adequate size and representative of the larger population (i.e. include people of all different sub-populations). The required sample size will depend on the expected size of the effect: if a small impact is expected, a larger sample is needed to achieve statistical significance in the results (Bhalerao and Kadam, 2010[154]).

3.3. Step 3a: Execute the evaluation study

A detailed execution plan is needed, which includes activities, timelines, resources needed and the individuals or entities responsible. In cases where resources or scientific research experience are scarce, it may be worth considering collaborating with a research organisation for data collection and analysis (e.g. academia, international organisation or private consultancy). Stakeholder engagement should be sought, to get buy-in for the plan and resources to execute the study – though it is not limited to this stage of the evaluation process (see Step 2, Section 2.2, for further details on engaging stakeholders).

The remainder of Step 3a provides details on executing an evaluation study – namely how to collect and analyse data.

3.3.1. Collect the data

Part of the execution plan should be the data collection procedures, which address issues such as logistics, consent, privacy, data security and other ethical considerations (see Box 3.10). Important questions to ask and answer in the data collection procedures (Centers for Disease Control and Prevention, 2012[151]; Olney and Barnes, 2013[153]; Public Health Ontario, 2016[132]).

- How is data collected, and how could this affect the results (e.g. would an email survey result in a higher response from computer-literate participants?)
- How do we recruit participants, in accordance with the desired study population previously defined?
- Who will be collecting the data, and how will they be trained for this task?
- How will we communicate the purpose of the study to potential participants?
- How will we obtain informed consent?
- How will data be stored safely?
- Is ethical approval required?

Box 3.10. Ethical considerations for evaluation studies

Informed consent

Informed consent is a process through which a prospective study participants voluntarily confirm their willingness to participate in the study, after having been fully informed about all the relevant aspects of the study (Manti and Licari, 2018[155]). Consent can be obtained in writing through a consent form, verbally prior to doing a telephone interview, or by clicking "next" on an online survey (Public Health Ontario, 2016[132]).

It is important to consider how informed consent can be obtained from people with intellectual disabilities (Horner-Johnson and Bailey, 2013[156]), underage persons (Vitiello, 2008[157]), vulnerable persons (Manti and Licari, 2018[155]) or people who are otherwise less able to understand the information presented or the implications of participation. It is possible to obtain consent from carers or family – called "informed consent by proxy" – though this may result in higher rates of refusal (Warren et al., 1986[158]) (Mason et al., 2006[159]).

Confidentiality

To encourage participants to share their personal information, confidentially needs to be assured (Public Health Ontario, 2016[132]). This can be done by full anonymisation of the data (where researchers or other staff cannot link responses to individuals), or by ensuring no personal data is available to anyone outside the study team. In addition, guidelines to ensure the safe storage of data need to be defined (Centers for Disease Control and Prevention, 2012[151]).

Sensitivity

The study needs to be sensitivity to participants' background, values and situation. Cultural sensitivity is based on awareness of cultural diversity (for example how culture may influence a participants values, beliefs and attitudes) and requires acknowledging and respecting these differences (Brooks, Manias and Bloomer, 2019[160]). Researchers should also consider whether the condition or behaviour they are looking at may be stigmatised, and how this could influence participation, participant experience and results (Millum et al., 2019[161]).

When to collect data depends on the intervention, its duration and the time after which outcomes are expected to become measurable. The following time points should be considered for data collection (Public Health Ontario, 2016[132]):

- **Start**: collect data at the start of an intervention and before any activities take place to get an accurate baseline – for both the intervention and the control group
- **During**: collect data throughout the intervention period instead of only at the end, to understand when the intervention is effective and observe trends such as participation levels
- **Completion and after**: collect data at the end of the intervention as well as some time after, to observe the longer-term impact and determine whether there is a lasting effect once the intervention has ended (see Box 3.11 for a real-world case study)

Box 3.11. Case study: Multimodal training intervention (Iceland) – collecting data

The Multimodal Training Intervention (MTI) is designed to improve the overall health of older individuals in Iceland through nutritional education information sessions and exercise classes. To assess the impact of MTI on participant outcomes, intervention administrators collected data for several indicators including BMI, blood pressure, physical activity, as well as scores on a range of endurance and strength tests. For each outcome of interest, data was collected at the start of the intervention, three times during the intervention (6-, 12- and 18-months) and upon completing the intervention.

Follow-up data was not collected (e.g. six months after conclusion of the intervention), which limits the ability to draw conclusions on the intervention's long-term impact. This is common amongst public health interventions given the lack of resources available to follow-up with intervention participants.

Source: Information provided by Janus Health Promotion.

Different timings may apply to different measures. For example, process measures should be monitored during the intervention, while the outcome indicator should at least be measured before and after the intervention.

For questionnaires or surveys, it is important to maximise the response rate (Olney and Barnes, 2013[153]). The response rate is the percentage of people targeted (those within the defined study population) that respond to the questionnaire. As this study population is defined with the aim of being of adequate size and representative, it is important that enough people within the study population participate to meet these two targets. A high overall rate of non-response could mean that the results are not statistically significant. If the non-response rate is higher in specific population groups, this could affect the accuracy of the results.

For surveys that are administered electronically, it is important to consider how the design and technology can affect the response rate (Box 3.12).

> **Box 3.12. Increasing the response rate for electronic surveys**
>
> Participation in electronic surveys and completion of questionnaires can be significantly increased using simple measures. Some examples are included below:
>
> - Ensure that the survey loads quickly
> - Allow participants to skip questions – to avoid them quitting the survey if they cannot answer one question
> - Give participants an estimation of the time required to complete, and monitor progress with progress bars
> - Scrolling may provide better completion rates than forcing respondents to click through pages with one or two questions
> - Start with easier yet interesting questions – saving complicated questions that may overwhelm and "boring" questions such as demographics for the end
>
> Source: Olney and Barnes (2013[153]), "Collecting and analyzing evaluation data – Planning and Evaluating Health Information Outreach Projects Booklet 3", https://nnlm.gov/nec/evalmaterials/bookletThree508.

3.3.2. Analyse the data

A first step in quantitative data analysis is the descriptive statistics (Olney and Barnes, 2013[153]). These descriptive or summary statistics are often averages or frequency counts, and provide an overview of the participant characteristics and the intervention results. Demographic and evaluation indicators can be presented for different population groups (e.g. by gender, age group, socio-economic status is highly recommended) or study arms (e.g. intervention and control group).

An important part of the initial descriptive analysis is to look at the pattern of missing data. Some participants may have dropped out of the study over time, or certain questions may have been left unanswered. If missing data are random (i.e. not related to the outcome of interest), it may not affect the results. However, it is possible that missing data is not random. For example, a sensitive question about alcohol consumption may be left blank by people who consume more alcohol and do not want to disclose this. Such a non-random pattern of missing data would change the results. It is therefore important to look at the degree and pattern of missing data, to try to understand whether the results could be affected. There are various techniques for dealing with missing data such as complete-case analysis (deleting observations with missing data) and substituting missing values with the mean and multiple imputation. The right technique will depend on the nature of the missing data (e.g. missing completely at random, at random or not at random).

After the descriptive analysis, different statistical analyses can be used to identify whether the observed effects are "real". There are statistical tests to compare outcomes in the intervention and control groups (or pre- and post-intervention), which determine whether a difference in outcome is statistically significant or whether it is likely to be due to chance. Where there are baseline differences between the intervention and control group that confound estimates of the effect of the intervention, regression-based methods can account for the confounders (such as age, gender and socio-economic factors), to see whether the intervention effect persists after controlling for these differences.

For qualitative data (for example from interviews or focus groups) there exist tried-and-tested analysis methods. The following steps suggest how large amounts of raw text data may be analysed (Olney and Barnes, 2013[153]):

- Prepare text files: this can be verbatim transcripts or summary records, and these will form the raw data
- Create a codebook: after reading through the text files, identify themes or categories and assign them a code. These codes can have multiple layers. For example, under the "issues" category there can be "lack of statistical expertise" and "lack of funding".
- Code the text: go through the text files and assign codes to sections of text. There are various software tools that can be used in this process (e.g. NVivo).
- Interpret the results: write summaries of the different categories. These summaries include a description of the broader theme and sub-themes, and can be supported with examples or quotes identified through the coded text.

This section represents a simplified overview of analysing data given it is not possible to provide a comprehensive overview of all statistical methods in this manual. The right statistical method will depend on many factors, including the type of indicators used, the structure of the data and the study design. For this reason, ensuring that statistical and analytical expertise is available for the analysis is crucial.

3.4. Step 3b: Act on evaluation results

Step 3b outlines possible follow-up actions after completing an evaluation as well as information on how to disseminate results.

3.4.1. Follow-up action

The results of the evaluation are not an end in and of themselves, rather they should be used as feedback to guide follow-up action. Specifically, evaluation results determine whether policy makers (Institute for Healthcare Improvement, n.d.[162]):

- **Adopt**: if the intervention is successful, it can be officially adopted and expanded to a wider population or for a longer time
- **Adapt**: if the evaluation identifies areas for improvement, the intervention should be adapted
- **Abandon**: if the intervention does not improve outcomes (or even worsens them) and no changes can be made to improve it, it may have to be abandoned.

To identify where improvements can be made, it is important to look at results across the entire logic model (Center for Community Health and Development, n.d.[163]). If issues were identified around inputs, activities and output (e.g. not enough participating practices, educational activities not completed), each should be reviewed with the aim of finding potential solutions or improvements. It is possible that the inputs, activities and outputs did not present clear issues, yet the intended outcomes were not met. In this case the basic design of intervention should be reviewed.

It is not always desirable to wait until the full results from the evaluation are available to make changes. If serious issues are identified mid-way through the evaluation period (for example a high drop-out rate), it would make sense to address this sooner rather than later (Center for Community Health and Development, n.d.[163]). However, this will affect the results of the study and should be taken note off during the analysis.

3.4.2. Disseminate results

Step 3, evaluate, culminates in the dissemination of evaluation results. Dissemination refers to the active spreading of evidence to a target audience via determined channels (Tabak et al., 2012[128]; Yuan et al., 2010[129]).

Disseminating evaluation results ensures lessons learnt reach interested stakeholders and can therefore be applied in future implementations. Where positive results ensue, disseminating evaluation findings can help gain stakeholder support for further scaling of the intervention (e.g. beyond the pilot study) or even transfer to a new target setting (see Box 3.13 for an example on disseminating results from Switzerland).

When disseminating results, it is important to keep in mind the target audience and tailor results accordingly. For example, when presenting to:

- **Payers**, it may be useful to compare the results of the evaluation with similar/competing interventions to highlight relative advantage
- **The public**, phrasing evaluation results in simple terms is appropriate, conversely, **experts** will likely be interested in the statistical analysis used to measure outcomes
- **Patients**, details on how the intervention affects patient outcomes will be of greater interest than potential cost savings, for example.

At this last stage of the evaluation, key political leaders and supported should be engaged to help promote and disseminate results.

Box 3.13. Case study: Sustainable spatial development (Switzerland) – disseminating results

The Swiss Federal Government supports a range of projects designed to test new approaches to implementing sustainable, social and exercise-friendly spatial developments. Support not only refers to financial assistance but also networking, counselling and co-ordination assistance. Over the period 2020-24, the Swiss Government plans to support 31 projects implemented across the country. To encourage exchange of information across implementation sites and other stakeholders, four different types of meetings are held (see Table 3.3).

Table 3.3. Process for disseminating results

Type of meeting	Purpose	Attendees	Frequency
Kick-off meeting	To kick-start the intervention and for project implementers to receive input from other stakeholders, such as experts	All intervention members (e.g. NGOs, city planners), relevant government personnel and experts	One meeting per intervention undertaken at the outset (1/5 years)
"Experience exchange" meeting	Opportunity for people across all interventions to come together to exchange experiences (e.g. "lessons-learned") and to discuss specific needs and experiences	Members from all interventions across a range of public health topics. Experts with a strong relation to the ongoing interventions	Once per year, per intervention
Mid-term "knowledge exchange" meeting	Similar to above, this is an opportunity to share experiences and hear about new developments	As above + additional experts from other disciplines, and possibly the public	Once meeting per intervention run 1/5 years
Final meeting	Used to showcase evaluation results from the intervention and thus showcase best practice	As above	Once at the end of the funding cycle for all projects combined

Source: Feedback provided directly by Swiss officials.

3.5. Conclusion of Step 3

The final section of the guidebook describes the steps for undertaking an evaluation – the design and execution of an evaluation study. The former, designing an evaluation study, although discussed in Step 3 of the guidebook (to cater to those solely interested in the evaluation component of the guidebook), should be undertaken once an intervention has been assessed as best practice and suitable for transfer (i.e. the end of Step 1). Designing the evaluation study at an early stage is necessary as it specifies the indicators and therefore the data needed to undertake an evaluation.

Execution of an evaluation study occurs once an intervention has been implemented (end of Step 2). It involves collecting primary and/or secondary sources of data to assess whether the intervention achieved its objectives. Data should be collected at the beginning and end of an intervention, and, if resources permit, a period after the intervention has concluded. Once collected, researchers must analyse the data, which includes choosing appropriate statistical methods to assess whether observed effects are due to the intervention or chance.

Results from the evaluation should guide follow-up action on whether to adopt, adapt or abandon the intervention. They should also be used to ensure lessons learned are applied to future implementations. Where positive result ensue, promoting evaluation findings can help gain support for scaling-up and/or transferring the intervention.

Additional tools and resources

Developing a logic model: Logic Model Workbook from Innovation Network (Innovation Network, n.d.[164]).

Theory of Change Guidance from the United Nations Development Group (United Nations Development Group, n.d.[165]).

Stakeholder engagement and other steps in programme evaluation: CDC's Introduction to Program Evaluation for Public Health Programs: A Self-Study Guide (2011[140]).

Data collection methods and other steps in programme evaluation: Public Health Ontario's Evaluating Health Promotion Programs: introductory workbook (Public Health Ontario, 2016[132]).

Developing an interview protocol: "Preparing for Interview Research: The Interview Protocol Refinement Framework" by Milagros Castillo-Montoya (2016[152]).

Collecting and analysing data: Collecting and analysing evaluation data – Planning and Evaluating Health Information Outreach Projects Booklet 3, by Olney and Barnes (2013[153]).

Acting on the results and other elements of community project evaluation: The Community Tool Box from the Center for Community Health and Development at the University of Kansas (Center for Community Health and Development, n.d.[163]).

Conclusion

Policy makers face increasing public health challenges caused by factors such as ageing populations, and changing environments and lifestyle behaviours. These challenges represent a health and economic burden, with those in worse health accruing higher health and labour costs, for example due to absenteeism from work. In response, policy makers are turning to evidence-based decisions to improve population health in a sustainable way.

The guidebook is designed to promote high-quality evidence-based decision making, by outlining a step-by-step process for selecting, implementing and evaluating best practice public health interventions. It can be used for all types of public health interventions, for this reason, information in the guidebook should be adapted to suit the specific needs of users.

Step 1, selecting an intervention, is broken into two key components: Step 1a) assesses whether an intervention is best practice while Step 1b) assesses whether the intervention can be transferred. Step 1a uses a MCDA framework consisting of five criteria to help policy makers identify best practice interventions: effectiveness, efficiency, equity, evidence-base and extent of coverage. For each criteria, the guidebook specifies several indicators to measure performance using, to the extent possible, those in international, publically available datasets. An intervention evaluated as best practice in one setting may not necessarily perform well in another setting due to the influence of external factors. Therefore, Step 1b outlines four contextual factors policy makers should consider to determine whether an intervention is transferable: the population, sector specific, political and economic contexts.

Once an intervention has been identified as best practice and appropriate for transfer, it must be implemented in the target setting. Step 2 of the guidebook provides a rationale for a formal implementation process and a step-by-step guide to implementation, illustrated with practical examples. Preparing implementation involves identifying people who actively contribute to implementation efforts; assessing resource needs, capacity and readiness to implement; as well as drafting an implementation protocol covering information such as timelines and management oversight. Step 2 also discusses the process for monitoring implementation as it unfolds, and the importance of supportive feedback loops and providing implementers with continual support.

Finally, Step 3 of the guidebook outlines how to evaluate the intervention in the target setting. This requires designing an evaluation study using a programme logic model, which specifies the inputs, activities, outputs and outcomes associated with an intervention. For each element within the logic model, realistic indicators must be chosen, that is, indicators for which there are available data and sufficient resources to collect and analyse the information. Data to measure performance against indicators can be used to undertake one of several evaluations, the most common being process and outcome evaluations. Finally, results from evaluations should guide follow-up action on whether to adopt, adapt or abandon the intervention. Results should also be used to ensure lessons learned are applied to future implementations and to build stakeholder support.

References

Ackermann, F. and C. Eden (2011), "Strategic Management of Stakeholders: Theory and Practice", *Long Range Planning*, Vol. 44/3, pp. 179-196, http://dx.doi.org/10.1016/j.lrp.2010.08.001. [113]

Barberan-Garcia, A. and I. Cano (2020), *Assessment of the Prehabilitation Unit at Hospital Clinic of Barcelona: period 2017-2019. NEXTCARE Implementation Report*. [121]

Barberan-Garcia, A. et al. (2018), "Protocol for regional implementation of collaborative self-management services to promote physical activity", *BMC Health Services Research*, Vol. 18/1, p. 560, http://dx.doi.org/10.1186/s12913-018-3363-8. [120]

Barnfield, A., N. Savolainen and A. Lounamaa (2020), "Health Promotion Interventions: Lessons from the Transfer of Good Practices in CHRODIS-PLUS", *International Journal of Environmental Research and Public Health*, Vol. 17/4, p. 1281, http://dx.doi.org/10.3390/ijerph17041281. [54]

Barnish, M. and S. Turner (2017), "The value of pragmatic and observational studies in health care and public health", *Pragmatic and Observational Research*, Vol. Volume 8, pp. 49-55, http://dx.doi.org/10.2147/por.s137701. [33]

Barry, M. et al. (eds.) (2019), *Implementing Mental Health Promotion*, Springer International Publishing, Cham, http://dx.doi.org/10.1007/978-3-030-23455-3. [110]

Berkman, N. et al. (2014), *The Empirical Evidence of Bias in Trials Measuring Treatment Differences*, Agency for Healthcare Research and Quality (US). [35]

Bhalerao, S. and P. Kadam (2010), "Sample size calculation", *International Journal of Ayurveda Research*, Vol. 1/1, p. 55, http://dx.doi.org/10.4103/0974-7788.59946. [154]

Bodkin, A. and S. Hakimi (2020), "Sustainable by design: a systematic review of factors for health promotion program sustainability", *BMC Public Health*, Vol. 20/1, http://dx.doi.org/10.1186/s12889-020-09091-9. [53]

Bonell, C. et al. (2006), *Assessment of generalisability in trials of health interventions: Suggested framework and systematic review*, British Medical Journal Publishing Group, http://dx.doi.org/10.1136/bmj.333.7563.346. [64]

Bonevski, B. et al. (2014), "Associations between alcohol, smoking, socioeconomic status and comorbidities: Evidence from the 45 and Up Study", *Drug and Alcohol Review*, Vol. 33/2, pp. 169-176, http://dx.doi.org/10.1111/dar.12104. [34]

Breitenstein, S. et al. (2010), "Implementation fidelity in community-based interventions", *Research in Nursing & Health*, Vol. 33/2, pp. n/a-n/a, http://dx.doi.org/10.1002/nur.20373. [102]

Brooks, J., K. Wilson and Z. Amir (2011), "Additional financial costs borne by cancer patients: A narrative review", *European Journal of Oncology Nursing*, Vol. 15/4, pp. 302-310, http://dx.doi.org/10.1016/j.ejon.2010.10.005. [81]

Brooks, L., E. Manias and M. Bloomer (2019), *Culturally sensitive communication in healthcare: A concept analysis*, Elsevier B.V., http://dx.doi.org/10.1016/j.colegn.2018.09.007. [160]

Brownson, R. et al. (2015), "Chapter 16: Implementation, Dissemination, and Diffusion of Public Health Interventions", in Glanz, K., B. Rimer and K. Viswanath (eds.), *Health Behavior: Theory, Research, and Practice*, Jossey-Bass. [99]

Burchett, H., M. Umoquit and M. Dobrow (2011), *How do we know when research from one setting can be useful in another? A review of external validity, applicability and transferability frameworks*, http://dx.doi.org/10.1258/jhsrp.2011.010124. [51]

Cambon, L. et al. (2013), "A tool to analyze the transferability of health promotion interventions.", *BMC public health*, Vol. 13, p. 1184, http://dx.doi.org/10.1186/1471-2458-13-1184. [82]

Canadian Public Health Association (2020), *Promising practices in Canada*, https://www.cpha.ca/promising-practices-canada (accessed on 24 March 2020). [16]

Carroll, C. et al. (2007), "A conceptual framework for implementation fidelity", *Implementation Science*, Vol. 2/1, p. 40, http://dx.doi.org/10.1186/1748-5908-2-40. [101]

Castillo-Montoya, M. (2016), "The Qualitative Report Preparing for Interview Research: The Interview Protocol Refinement Framework", *The Qualitative Report*, Vol. 21/5, pp. 811-831, https://nsuworks.nova.edu/tqr/vol21/iss5/2 (accessed on 3 April 2020). [152]

CDC (2018), *Program Evaluation Framework Checklist*, https://www.cdc.gov/eval/steps/step2/index.htm (accessed on 30 March 2020). [137]

CDC (2011), *Program Evaluation Tip Sheet: Reach and impact*, https://www.cdc.gov/dhdsp/programs/spha/docs/reach_impact_tip_sheet.pdf (accessed on 21 April 2020). [43]

Center for Community Health and Development (n.d.), *Community Tool Box: Chapter 39. Using Evaluation to Understand and Improve the Initiative. Section 3. Refining the Program or Intervention Based on Evaluation Research*, https://ctb.ku.edu/en/table-of-contents/evaluate/evaluate-community-interventions/refine-intervention/main (accessed on 28 May 2020). [163]

Centers for Disease Control and Prevention (2016), *CDC approach to evaluation*, https://www.cdc.gov/eval/approach/index.htm. [134]

Centers for Disease Control and Prevention (2012), *Introduction to Program Evaluation for Public Health Programs: A Self-Study Guide*, https://www.cdc.gov/eval/guide/index.htm (accessed on 8 May 2021). [151]

Centers for Disease Control and Prevention (2011), *Introduction to Program Evaluation for Public Health Programs: A Self-Study Guide*, Centers for Disease Control and Prevention, Atlanta, GA, https://www.cdc.gov/eval/guide/CDCEvalManual.pdf (accessed on 31 March 2020). [140]

Centre for Epidemiology and Evidence (2017), *Developing and Using Program Logic: A Guide*, Evidence and Evaluation Guidance Series, Population and Public Health Division. Ministry of Health, https://www.health.nsw.gov.au/research/Publications/developing-program-logic.pdf. [135]

CHRODIS (2017), *Recommendations report on applicability and transferability of practices into different settings and countries*, http://chrodis.eu/wp-content/uploads/2014/10/170223_wp5-t5_report-successfactorstransf-scalability_wotable2.pdf. [56]

CHRODIS (2015), *Task 1: selecting JA-CHRODIS criteria to assess good practice in interventions related to chronic conditions*, http://chrodis.eu/wp-content/uploads/2016/03/Delphi-2_MULTIMORBID.pdf. [22]

Clarke, G. et al. (2019), "Evaluating the impact of healthcare interventions using routine data", *BMJ*, p. l2239, http://dx.doi.org/10.1136/bmj.l2239. [145]

Cookson, R. et al. (2016), "Health Equity Indicators for the English NHS: a longitudinal whole-population study at the small-area level", *Health Services and Delivery Research*, Vol. 4/26, pp. 1-224, http://dx.doi.org/10.3310/hsdr04260. [31]

Cookson, R., M. Drummond and H. Weatherly (2009), "Explicit incorporation of equity considerations into economic evaluation of public health interventions", *Health Economics, Policy and Law*, Vol. 4/2, pp. 231-245, http://dx.doi.org/10.1017/S1744133109004903. [30]

Craig, P. et al. (2008), "Developing and evaluating complex interventions: the new Medical Research Council guidance.", *BMJ (Clinical research ed.)*, Vol. 337, p. a1655, http://dx.doi.org/10.1136/bmj.a1655. [47]

Cuijpers, P., I. De Graaf and E. Bohlmeijer (2005), "Adapting and disseminating effective public health interventions in another country: Towards a systematic approach", *European Journal of Public Health*, Vol. 15/2, pp. 166-169, http://dx.doi.org/10.1093/eurpub/cki124. [63]

de Waard, A. et al. (2018), "Barriers and facilitators to participation in a health check for cardiometabolic diseases in primary care: A systematic review", *European Journal of Preventive Cardiology*, Vol. 25/12, pp. 1326-1340, http://dx.doi.org/10.1177/2047487318780751. [125]

Deaton, A. and N. Cartwright (2018), "Understanding and misunderstanding randomized controlled trials", *Social Science & Medicine*, Vol. 210, pp. 2-21, http://dx.doi.org/10.1016/j.socscimed.2017.12.005. [32]

Devlin, N. and J. Sussex (2011), *Incorporating multiple criteria in HTA*, Office of Health Economics, London. [3]

Diepeveen, S. et al. (2013), "Public acceptability of government intervention to change health-related behaviours: A systematic review and narrative synthesis", *BMC Public Health*, Vol. 13/1, p. 756, http://dx.doi.org/10.1186/1471-2458-13-756. [68]

Durlak, J. and E. DuPre (2008), "Implementation Matters: A Review of Research on the Influence of Implementation on Program Outcomes and the Factors Affecting Implementation", *American Journal of Community Psychology*, Vol. 41/3-4, pp. 327-350, http://dx.doi.org/10.1007/s10464-008-9165-0. [97]

Effective Public Health Pratice Project (1998), *Quality assessment tool for quantitative studies*, https://www.nccmt.ca/knowledge-repositories/search/14. [36]

Engbers, L. and J. Sattelmair (2008), *Monitoring and Evaluation of Worksite Health Promotion Programs - Current state of knowledge and implications for practice*, World Health Organization, https://www.who.int/dietphysicalactivity/Engbers-monitoringevaluation.pdf. [141]

Escoffery, C. et al. (2018), "A systematic review of adaptations of evidence-based public health interventions globally", *Implementation science : IS*, Vol. 13/1, p. 125, http://dx.doi.org/10.1186/s13012-018-0815-9. [94]

European Commission (2021), *Public Health Best Practice Portal*, https://webgate.ec.europa.eu/dyna/bp-portal/ (accessed on 4 October 2021). [20]

European Commission (2015), *European scaling-up strategy in active & healthy ageing*, Ageing, The European Innovation Partnership on Active and Health, https://ec.europa.eu/research/innovation-union/pdf/active-healthy-ageing/scaling_up_strategy.pdf. [55]

European Commission (n.d.), *Criteria to select best practices in health promotion and chronic disease prevention and management in Europe*, https://ec.europa.eu/health/sites/health/files/major_chronic_diseases/docs/sgpp_bestpracticescriteria_en.pdf. [21]

European Commission (n.d.), *Submitter's guide: best pratice portal*, https://webgate.ec.europa.eu/dyna/bp-portal/SubmittersGuide.pdf. [46]

European Commission Directorate General for Health and Food Safety (2017), *Criteria to select best practices in health promotion and chronic disease prevention and management in Europe*, https://ec.europa.eu/health/sites/health/files/major_chronic_diseases/docs/sgpp_bestpracticescriteria_en.pdf. [23]

Fixsen, D. et al. (2005), *Implementation research: a synthesis of the literature*, University of South Florida, Louis de la Parte Florida Mental Health Institute, The National Implementation Research Network (FMHI Publication 231). [127]

Frazão, T. et al. (2018), *Multicriteria decision analysis (MCDA) in health care: A systematic review of the main characteristics and methodological steps*, BioMed Central Ltd., http://dx.doi.org/10.1186/s12911-018-0663-1. [9]

Frieden, T. (2014), "Six components necessary for effective public health program implementation.", *American Journal of Public Health*, Vol. 104/1, pp. 17-22, http://dx.doi.org/10.2105/AJPH.2013.301608. [87]

Fullaondo, A., J. Txarramendieta and E. De Manuel (2018), *Guideline on Implementation Strategy. Module I: Pre-Implementation phase*, European Commission, Brussels. [104]

Ghandour, R. et al. (2014), "Priority setting for the prevention and control of cardiovascular diseases: multi-criteria decision analysis in four eastern Mediterranean countries", *International Journal of Public Health*, Vol. 60/S1, pp. 73-81, http://dx.doi.org/10.1007/s00038-014-0569-3. [167]

Gimeno Miguel, A. et al. (2020), *WP6: Pilot implementation of the CHRODIS IMCM in Aragón for improving care of patients with multimorbidity Implementation Report*. [111]

Greenhalgh, T. et al. (2004), "Diffusion of innovations in service organizations: Systematic review and recommendations", *The Milbank Quarterly*, Vol. 82/4, pp. 581-629, http://dx.doi.org/10.1111/j.0887-378X.2004.00325.x. [126]

Griffiths, J., H. Maggs and E. George (2008), *Stakeholder Involvement: Background paper prepared for the WHO/WEF Joint Event on Preventing Noncommunicable Diseases in the Workplace (Dalian/ China, September 2007)*, World Health Organization, Geneva. [114]

Gunnarsdóttir, G. and G. Ingibjörg (2020), *Wellbeing for all – Improved quality and sustainability of the Health Promoting Community programme in Iceland using innovative practical approach to implement selected parts of the JOGG programme and utilising the JA CHRODIS+ National Policy dialogue (WP*, Directorate of Health Iceland. [59]

Guyatt, G. et al. (2011), "GRADE guidelines: 1. Introduction - GRADE evidence profiles and summary of findings tables", *Journal of Clinical Epidemiology*, Vol. 64/4, pp. 383-394, http://dx.doi.org/10.1016/j.jclinepi.2010.04.026. [37]

Haacker, M., T. Hallett and R. Atun (2019), "On discount rates for economic evaluations in global health", *Health Policy and Planning*, http://dx.doi.org/10.1093/heapol/czz127. [147]

Horner-Johnson, W. and D. Bailey (2013), "Assessing Understanding and Obtaining Consent From Adults With Intellectual Disabilities for a Health Promotion Study", *Journal of Policy and Practice in Intellectual Disabilities*, Vol. 10/3, pp. 260-265, http://dx.doi.org/10.1111/jppi.12048. [156]

Hussein, I. et al. (2020), *Health and wellbeing for all – development and implementation of a culturally sensitive lifestyle intervention for Somalis in Finland through the adoption of JA CHRODIS recommendations and set of criteria*, European Commission, Brussels. [123]

Innovation Network (n.d.), *Logic Model Workbook*, http://www.pointk.org/client_docs/File/logic_model_workbook.pdf (accessed on 19 August 2019). [164]

Institute for Healthcare Improvement (n.d.), *Plan-Do-Study-Act (PDSA) Worksheet*, http://www.ihi.org/resources/Pages/Tools/PlanDoStudyActWorksheet.aspx (accessed on 8 May 2021). [162]

International Council of Nurses et al. (2008), *Guidelines: Incentives for health professionals*, http://www.whpa.org/sites/default/files/2018-11/WHPA-positive_practice_environments-guidelines-EN.pdf (accessed on 4 September 2020). [115]

Irving, M. et al. (2016), "A Critical Review of Grading Systems: Implications for Public Health Policy", *Evaluation & the Health Professions*, Vol. 40/2, pp. 244-262, http://dx.doi.org/10.1177/0163278716645161. [38]

Iwelunmor, J., V. Newsome and C. Airhihenbuwa (2014), "Framing the impact of culture on health: A systematic review of the PEN-3 cultural model and its application in public health research and interventions", *Ethnicity and Health*, Vol. 19/1, pp. 20-46, http://dx.doi.org/10.1080/13557858.2013.857768. [73]

JA-CHRODIS (2017), *Joint Action on Chronic Diseases and Promoting Healthy Ageing across the Life Cycle (JA-CHRODIS). Work Package 5: Good practices in the field of health promotion and chronic disease prevention across the life cycle. Recommendations report on applicability*, http://chrodis.eu/wp-content/uploads/2014/10/170223_wp5-t5_report-successfactorstransf-scalability_wotable2.pdf. [60]

Jenkins, C. (2003), *Building a better health: A handbook of behavioral change*, Pan American Health Organization, Washington DC, https://www.paho.org/hq/dmdocuments/2010/9275115907_reduce.pdf. [96]

Kaló, Z. et al. (2020), "Development of transferability guidance for integrated care models with special focus on Central and Eastern European countries", *Croatian Medical Journal*, Vol. 61/3, pp. 252-259, http://dx.doi.org/10.3325/cmj.2020.61.252. [95]

Kidholm, K. et al. (2012), "A model for assessment of telemedicine applications: Mast", *International Journal of Technology Assessment in Health Care*, Vol. 28/1, pp. 44-51, http://dx.doi.org/10.1017/S0266462311000638. [92]

Kidholm, K. et al. (2012), "A model for assessment of telemedicine applications: Mast", *International Journal of Technology Assessment in Health Care*, Vol. 28/1, pp. 44-51, http://dx.doi.org/10.1017/S0266462311000638. [62]

Lehne, G. et al. (2019), "Equity impact assessment of interventions to promote physical activity among older adults: A logic model framework", *International Journal of Environmental Research and Public Health*, Vol. 16/3, http://dx.doi.org/10.3390/ijerph16030420. [24]

Leschied, A., D. Saklofske and G. Flett (eds.) (2018), "Handbook of School-Based Mental Health Promotion An Evidence-Informed Framework for Implementation", Springer, http://dx.doi.org/10.1007/978-3-319-89842-1_1. [109]

Lobo, R., M. Petrich and S. Burns (2014), "Supporting health promotion practitioners to undertake evaluation for program development", *BMC Public Health*, Vol. 14/1, http://dx.doi.org/10.1186/1471-2458-14-1315. [131]

Lupiañez-Villanueva, F., A. Sachinopoulou and A. Thebe (2015), *Strategic Intelligence Monitor on Personal Health Systems Phase 3 (SIMPHS3): Oulu Self-Care (Finland) Case Study Report*, European Commission JRC Science and Policy Reports, https://publications.jrc.ec.europa.eu/repository/bitstream/JRC94492/jrc94492.pdf. [76]

Malden, S. et al. (2020), "Assessing the acceptability of an adapted preschool obesity prevention programme: ToyBox-Scotland", *Child: Care, Health and Development*, Vol. 46/2, pp. 213-222, http://dx.doi.org/10.1111/cch.12736. [78]

Mandelblatt, J. et al. (2017), "Evaluating Frameworks That Provide Value Measures for Health Care Interventions", *Value in Health*, Vol. 20/2, pp. 185-192, http://dx.doi.org/10.1016/j.jval.2016.11.013. [8]

Mandel, U., A. Derx and F. Ilzkovitz (2008), *The effectiveness and efficiency of public spending*, European Commission, https://ec.europa.eu/economy_finance/publications/pages/publication11902_en.pdf. [14]

Mann, C. (2003), *Observational research methods. Research design II: Cohort, cross sectional, and case-control studies*, British Association for Accident and Emergency Medicine, http://dx.doi.org/10.1136/emj.20.1.54. [40]

Manti, S. and A. Licari (2018), "How to obtain informed consent for research", *Breathe*, Vol. 14/2, pp. 145-152, http://dx.doi.org/10.1183/20734735.001918. [155]

Marsh, K. et al. (2013), "Prioritizing investments in public health: a multi-criteria decision analysis", *Journal of Public Health*, Vol. 35/3, pp. 460-466, http://dx.doi.org/10.1093/pubmed/fds099. [44]

Mason, S. et al. (2006), "Brief report on the experience of using proxy consent for incapacitated adults", *Journal of Medical Ethics*, Vol. 32/1, pp. 61-62, http://dx.doi.org/10.1136/jme.2005.012302. [159]

McCannon, C., M. Schall and R. Perla (2008), *Planning for Scale: A Guide for Designing Large-Scale Improvement Initiatives. IHI Innovation Series white paper*, Institute for Healthcare Improvement, Cambridge, Massachusetts, http://www.IHI.org. [74]

Meyers, D., J. Durlak and A. Wandersman (2012), "The Quality Implementation Framework: A Synthesis of Critical Steps in the Implementation Process", *American Journal of Community Psychology*, Vol. 50/3-4, pp. 462-480, http://dx.doi.org/10.1007/s10464-012-9522-x. [103]

Millum, J. et al. (2019), "Ethical challenges in global health-related stigma research", *BMC Medicine*, Vol. 17/1, p. 84, http://dx.doi.org/10.1186/s12916-019-1317-6. [161]

Movsisyan, A. et al. (2019), *Adapting evidence-informed complex population health interventions for new contexts: A systematic review of guidance*, BioMed Central Ltd., http://dx.doi.org/10.1186/s13012-019-0956-5. [93]

Mühlbacher, A. and A. Kaczynski (2016), "Making Good Decisions in Healthcare with Multi-Criteria Decision Analysis: The Use, Current Research and Future Development of MCDA", *Applied Health Economics and Health Policy*, Vol. 14/1, pp. 29-40, http://dx.doi.org/10.1007/s40258-015-0203-4. [6]

Napier, A. et al. (2014), "Culture and health", *The Lancet*, Vol. 384/9954, pp. 1607-1639, http://dx.doi.org/10.1016/S0140-6736(14)61603-2. [71]

Napier, D. et al. (2017), *Culture matters: using a cultural contexts of health approach to enhance policy-making (Policy brief, No. 1)*, World Health Organisation Regional Office for Europe, http://www.euro.who.int/__data/assets/pdf_file/0009/334269/14780_World-Health-Organisation_Context-of-Health_TEXT-AW-WEB.pdf?ua=1. [70]

National Collaborating Centre for Methods and Tools (2007), *Tool for Assessing Applicability and Transferability of Evidence*, https://www.nccmt.ca/uploads/media/media/0001/01/a13748201ebe5a6793cc641b109e21c70307dfdc.pdf. [85]

National Institute for Health and Care Excellence (2020), *Glossary*, https://www.nice.org.uk/glossary?letter=e (accessed on 24 March 2020). [12]

NEJM (2020), "Social Determinants of Health (SDOH)", *NEJM Catalyst Carryover*, Vol. 3/6, http://dx.doi.org/10.1056/CAT.17.0312. [25]

Ng, E. and P. de Colombani (2015), "Framework for Selecting Best Practices in Public Health: A Systematic Literature Review.", *Journal of Public Health Research*, Vol. 4/3, p. 577, http://dx.doi.org/10.4081/jphr.2015.577. [2]

Nilsen, P. (2015), "Making sense of implementation theories, models and frameworks", *Implementation Science*, Vol. 10/1, p. 53, http://dx.doi.org/10.1186/s13012-015-0242-0. [98]

Norris, S. et al. (2019), "Complex health interventions in complex systems: improving the process and methods for evidence-informed health decisions", *BMJ Global Health*, Vol. 4/Suppl 1, p. e000963, http://dx.doi.org/10.1136/bmjgh-2018-000963. [48]

O'Connor-Fleming, M. et al. (2006), "A framework for evaluating health promotion programs", *Health Promotion Journal of Australia*, Vol. 17/1, pp. 61-66, http://dx.doi.org/10.1071/he06061. [130]

OECD (2020), *How's Life? 2020: Measuring Well-being*, OECD Publishing, Paris, https://dx.doi.org/10.1787/9870c393-en. [138]

OECD (2020), *OECD Main Economic Indicators (MEI)*, https://www.oecd.org/sdd/oecdmaineconomicindicatorsmei.htm (accessed on 24 March 2020). [90]

OECD (2019), *Health at a Glance 2019: OECD Indicators*, OECD Publishing, Paris, https://dx.doi.org/10.1787/4dd50c09-en. [84]

OECD (2019), *The Heavy Burden of Obesity: The Economics of Prevention*, OECD Health Policy Studies, OECD Publishing, Paris, https://dx.doi.org/10.1787/67450d67-en. [1]

OECD (2014), *Lobbyists, Governments and Public Trust Volume 3: Implementing the OECD Principles for Transparency and Integrity in Lobbying*, OECD, Paris, https://www.oecd.org/gov/ethics/lobbyists-governments-trust-vol-3-highlights.pdf. [88]

OECD Health Statistics (2017), *Health status*, OECD Publishing, Paris, https://stats.oecd.org/BrandedView.aspx?oecd_bv_id=health-data-en&doi=data-00349-en. [18]

OECD.Stat (2019), *Health expenditure and financing*, OECD Publishing, Paris, https://stats.oecd.org/Index.aspx?DataSetCode=SHA# (accessed on 24 March 2020). [91]

OECD/European Union (2018), *Health at a Glance: Europe 2018: State of Health in the EU Cycle*, OECD Publishing, Paris/European Union, Brussels, https://dx.doi.org/10.1787/health_glance_eur-2018-en. [83]

OECD and European Commission (2008), *Handbook on constructing composite indicators: methodology and user guide*, OECD (the Statistics Directorate and the Directorate for Science, Technology and Industry) and the Applied Statistics and Econometrics Unit of the Joint Research Centre (JRC) of the European Commission, https://www.oecd.org/sdd/42495745.pdf. [45]

Olney, C. and S. Barnes (2013), *Collecting and analyzing evaluation data - Planning and Evaluating Health Information Outreach Projects Booklet 3*, National Network of Libraries of Medicine. [153]

Oxford University (2016), *OCEBM Levels of Evidence*, https://www.cebm.net/2016/05/ocebm-levels-of-evidence/. [41]

Palmer, K. et al. (2019), *A Methodological Approach for Implementing an Integrated Multimorbidity Care Model: Results from the Pre-Implementation Stage of Joint Action CHRODIS-PLUS*, p. 5044, http://dx.doi.org/10.3390/ijerph16245044. [105]

Peters, D. et al. (2014), "Republished research: Implementation research: What it is and how to do it", *British Journal of Sports Medicine*, Vol. 48/8, pp. 731-736, http://dx.doi.org/10.1136/bmj.f6753. [117]

Pettitt, D. and S. Raza (2016), "The Limitations of QALY: A Literature Review", *Journal of Stem Cell Research & Therapy*, Vol. 06/04, http://dx.doi.org/10.4172/2157-7633.1000334. [17]

Phelps, C. and G. Madhavan (2017), "Using Multicriteria Approaches to Assess the Value of Health Care", *Value in Health*, Vol. 20/2, pp. 251-255, http://dx.doi.org/10.1016/j.jval.2016.11.011. [7]

Phillips, S. (2005), *Defining and measuring gender: A social determinant of health whose time has come*, BioMed Central, http://dx.doi.org/10.1186/1475-9276-4-11. [29]

Pihlajamäki, J. et al. (2019), "Digitally supported program for type 2 diabetes risk identification and risk reduction in real-world setting: Protocol for the StopDia model and randomized controlled trial", *BMC Public Health*, Vol. 19/1, pp. 1-13, http://dx.doi.org/10.1186/s12889-019-6574-y. [124]

Piletič, M. et al. (2020), *WP7- Slovenia Individual pilot action report*, http://chrodis.eu/wp-content/uploads/2020/07/a-final-t7.2-slovenia.docx. [112]

Proctor, E. et al. (2011), "Outcomes for implementation research: Conceptual distinctions, measurement challenges, and research agenda", *Administration and Policy in Mental Health and Mental Health Services Research*, Vol. 38/2, pp. 65-76, http://dx.doi.org/10.1007/s10488-010-0319-7. [118]

Productivity Commission (2020), *Report on Government Services 2020*, https://www.pc.gov.au/research/ongoing/report-on-government-services/2020/approach/performance-measurement (accessed on 24 March 2020). [13]

Promberger, M. and T. Marteau (2013), "When do financial incentives reduce intrinsic motivation? Comparing behaviors studied in psychological and economic literatures", *Health Psychology*, Vol. 32/9, pp. 950-957, http://dx.doi.org/10.1037/a0032727. [116]

Public Health Ontario (2016), *Evaluating health promotion programs: introductory workbook*, https://www.publichealthontario.ca/-/media/documents/E/2016/evaluating-hp-programs-workbook.pdf?la=en. [132]

Public Health Ontario (2016), *Focus On: Logic model–A planning and evaluation tool*, https://www.publichealthontario.ca/-/media/documents/F/2016/focus-on-logic-model.pdf?la=en. [136]

Public Health Ontario (2015), *Priority Populations Project: Understanding and Identifying Priority Populations for Public Health in Ontario*, https://www.publichealthontario.ca/-/media/documents/priority-populations-technical.pdf?la=en (accessed on 20 April 2020). [26]

Rasmussen, B. et al. (2015), "A qualitative study of the key factors in implementing telemedical monitoring of diabetic foot ulcer patients", *International Journal of Medical Informatics*, Vol. 84/10, pp. 799-807, http://dx.doi.org/10.1016/j.ijmedinf.2015.05.012. [122]

RE-AIM (2020), *REACH*, http://www.re-aim.org/about/what-is-re-aim/reach/. [11]

Reddy, B. et al. (2016), "Using MCDA to generate and interpret evidence to inform local government investment in public health", *EURO Journal on Decision Processes*, Vol. 4/3-4, pp. 161-181, http://dx.doi.org/10.1007/s40070-016-0059-3. [168]

Reeve, C., J. Humphreys and J. Wakerman (2015), "A comprehensive health service evaluation and monitoring framework", *Evaluation and Program Planning*, Vol. 53, pp. 91-98, http://dx.doi.org/10.1016/j.evalprogplan.2015.08.006. [166]

Rehfuess, E., N. Bruce and A. Pruss-Ustun (2011), "GRADE for the advancement of public health", *Journal of Epidemiology & Community Health*, Vol. 65/6, pp. 559-559, http://dx.doi.org/10.1136/jech.2010.130013. [39]

Rice, N. and P. Smith (2001), "Ethics and geographical equity in health care", *Journal of Medical Ethics*, Vol. 27/4, pp. 256-261, http://dx.doi.org/10.1136/jme.27.4.256. [80]

Rose, G., K. Khaw and M. Marmot (2008), *Rose's Strategy of Preventive Medicine*, Oxford University Press, http://dx.doi.org/10.1093/acprof:oso/9780192630971.001.0001. [89]

Rychetnik, L. et al. (2002), "Criteria for evaluating evidence on public health interventions.", *Journal of epidemiology and community health*, Vol. 56/2, pp. 119-27, http://dx.doi.org/10.1136/jech.56.2.119. [5]

Sanson-Fisher, R. et al. (2007), "Limitations of the Randomized Controlled Trial in Evaluating Population-Based Health Interventions", *American Journal of Preventive Medicine*, Vol. 33/2, pp. 155-161, http://dx.doi.org/10.1016/j.amepre.2007.04.007. [142]

Saracutu, M. et al. (2018), "Protocol for a feasibility and acceptability study using a brief ACT-based intervention for people from Southwest Wales who live with persistent pain", *BMJ Open*, Vol. 8/11, p. e021866, http://dx.doi.org/10.1136/bmjopen-2018-021866. [69]

Sassi, F. (2006), "Calculating QALYs, comparing QALY and DALY calculations.", *Health policy and planning*, Vol. 21/5, pp. 402-8, http://dx.doi.org/10.1093/heapol/czl018. [19]

Saunders, R., M. Evans and P. Joshi (2005), "Developing a Process-Evaluation Plan for Assessing Health Promotion Program Implementation: A How-To Guide", *Health Promotion Practice*, Vol. 6/2, pp. 134-147, http://dx.doi.org/10.1177/1524839904273387. [119]

Schloemer, T. and P. Schröder-Bäck (2018), "Criteria for evaluating transferability of health interventions: a systematic review and thematic synthesis", *Implementation Science*, Vol. 13/1, p. 88, http://dx.doi.org/10.1186/s13012-018-0751-8. [49]

SCIROCCO (n.d.), *Maturity Model*, https://www.scirocco-project.eu/maturitymodel/ (accessed on 9 December 2020). [79]

Sekhon, M., M. Cartwright and J. Francis (2017), "Acceptability of healthcare interventions: An overview of reviews and development of a theoretical framework", *BMC Health Services Research*, Vol. 17/1, p. 88, http://dx.doi.org/10.1186/s12913-017-2031-8. [66]

SELFIE 2020 (2017), *Working Package 4: Development of an analytical framework to perform a comprehensive evaluation of integrated care programmes for multi-morbidity using Multi-Criteria Decision Analysis*, European Commission. [10]

Snijder, M. et al. (2017), "Cohort profile: The Healthy Life in an Urban Setting (HELIUS) study in Amsterdam, the Netherlands", *BMJ Open*, Vol. 7/12, p. e017873, http://dx.doi.org/10.1136/bmjopen-2017-017873. [28]

Spencer, L. et al. (2013), "Seeking best practices: a conceptual framework for planning and improving evidence-based practices.", *Preventing chronic disease*, Vol. 10, p. E207, http://dx.doi.org/10.5888/pcd10.130186. [15]

Stegeman, I. et al. (2020), *D5.3 Recommendations for the implementation of health promotion good practices: Building on what works: transferring and implementing good practice to strengthen health promotion and disease prevention in Europe*, EuroHealthNet & Finnish Institute for Health and Welfare. [58]

Stok, F. et al. (2016), "Hungry for an intervention? Adolescent's ratings of acceptability of eating-related intervention strategies", *BMC Public Health*, Vol. 16/1, p. 5, http://dx.doi.org/10.1186/s12889-015-2665-6. [67]

Suthers, R., M. Broom and E. Beck (2018), "Key Characteristics of Public Health Interventions Aimed at Increasing Whole Grain Intake: A Systematic Review", *Journal of Nutrition Education and Behavior*, Vol. 50/8, pp. 813-823, http://dx.doi.org/10.1016/j.jneb.2018.05.013. [57]

Tabak, R. et al. (2012), *Bridging research and practice: Models for dissemination and implementation research*, Elsevier Inc., http://dx.doi.org/10.1016/j.amepre.2012.05.024. [128]

Tan-Torres Edejer, T. et al. (2003), *WHO Guide to cost-effectiveness analysis*, https://www.who.int/choice/publications/p_2003_generalised_cea.pdf (accessed on 2 September 2019). [146]

Tao, W., J. Agerholm and B. Burström (2016), "The impact of reimbursement systems on equity in access and quality of primary care: A systematic literature review", *BMC Health Services Research*, Vol. 16/1, pp. 1-10, http://dx.doi.org/10.1186/s12913-016-1805-8. [77]

The Better Care Fund (2015), *How to... understand and measure impact*, https://www.england.nhs.uk/wp-content/uploads/2015/06/bcf-user-guide-04.pdf.pdf (accessed on 31 March 2020). [133]

Thiese, M. (2014), "Observational and interventional study design types; an overview", *Biochemia Medica*, Vol. 24/2, pp. 199-210, http://dx.doi.org/10.11613/BM.2014.022. [143]

Thokala, P. et al. (2016), "Multiple Criteria Decision Analysis for Health Care Decision Making—An Introduction: Report 1 of the ISPOR MCDA Emerging Good Practices Task Force", *Value in Health*, Vol. 19/1, pp. 1-13, http://dx.doi.org/10.1016/J.JVAL.2015.12.003. [4]

Trompette, J. et al. (2014), "Stakeholders' perceptions of transferability criteria for health promotion interventions: A case study", *BMC Public Health*, Vol. 14/1, pp. 1-11, http://dx.doi.org/10.1186/1471-2458-14-1134. [50]

U.S. Preventive Services Taskforce (2017), *Section 4. Evidence Review Development*, https://www.uspreventiveservicestaskforce.org/uspstf/section-4-evidence-review-development (accessed on 31 March 2020). [42]

United Nations Development Group (n.d.), *Theory of Change: UNDAF companion guide*, https://unsdg.un.org/sites/default/files/UNDG-UNDAF-Companion-Pieces-7-Theory-of-Change.pdf. [165]

Victorian Government Department of Health (2010), *Evaluation framework for health promotion and disease prevention programs*, https://www2.health.vic.gov.au/Api/downloadmedia/%7BCD822DEB-053E-435C-B3AB-2EC7DCF4FB92%7D. [139]

Vitiello, B. (2008), "Effectively Obtaining Informed Consent for Child and Adolescent Participation in Mental Health Research", *Ethics & Behavior*, Vol. 18/2-3, pp. 182-198, http://dx.doi.org/10.1080/10508420802064234. [157]

Walker, R., J. Strom Williams and L. Egede (2016), "Influence of Race, Ethnicity and Social Determinants of Health on Diabetes Outcomes", *American Journal of the Medical Sciences*, Vol. 351/4, pp. 366-373, http://dx.doi.org/10.1016/j.amjms.2016.01.008. [27]

Wandersman, A. et al. (2008), "Bridging the gap between prevention research and practice: The interactive systems framework for dissemination and implementation", *American Journal of Community Psychology*, Vol. 41/3-4, pp. 171-181, http://dx.doi.org/10.1007/s10464-008-9174-z. [100]

Wang, S., J. Moss and J. Hiller (2006), "Applicability and transferability of interventions in evidence-based public health.", *Health promotion international*, Vol. 21/1, pp. 76-83, http://dx.doi.org/10.1093/heapro/dai025. [52]

Warren, J. et al. (1986), "Informed Consent by Proxy", *New England Journal of Medicine*, Vol. 315/18, pp. 1124-1128, http://dx.doi.org/10.1056/NEJM198610303151804. [158]

Weijer, C. et al. (2011), "Ethical issues posed by cluster randomized trials in health research", *Trials*, Vol. 12/1, http://dx.doi.org/10.1186/1745-6215-12-100. [144]

WHO (2020), *Metrics: Disability-Adjusted Life Year (DALY)*, World Health Organization Geneva, https://www.who.int/healthinfo/global_burden_disease/metrics_daly/en/ (accessed on 26 March 2020). [171]

WHO (2018), *Healthy Diet*, World Health Organization Geneva, https://www.who.int/health-topics/healthy-diet#tab=tab_1. [170]

WHO (2011), *Identifying and addressing barriers to implementing policy options. In: SURE guides for preparing and using evidence-based policy briefs*, World Health Organization, Geneva, https://epoc.cochrane.org/sites/epoc.cochrane.org/files/public/uploads/SURE-Guides-v2.1/Collectedfiles/sure_guides.html. [61]

WHO (2010), *Creating an enabling environment for population-based salt reduction strategies: eport of a joint technical meeting held by WHO and the Food Standards Agency, United Kingdom, July 2010*, World Health Organization, https://apps.who.int/iris/handle/10665/44474. [106]

WHO (2010), *Set of Recommendations on the Marketing of Foods and Non-Alcoholic Beverages to Children*, World Health Organization, Geneva, https://apps.who.int/iris/rest/bitstreams/52869/retrieve. [107]

WHO (n.d.), *Health systems: Governance*, World Health Organization, Geneva, https://www.who.int/healthsystems/topics/stewardship/en/ (accessed on 12 May 2020). [75]

WHO Regional Office for Europe (n.d.), *Cultural contexts of health and well-being*, World Health Organization, Geneva, http://www.euro.who.int/en/data-and-evidence/cultural-contexts-of-health-and-well-being (accessed on 9 March 2020). [72]

WHO; ExpandNet (2009), *Practical guidance for scaling up health service innovations*, World Health Organization, Geneva, https://expandnet.net/PDFs/WHO_ExpandNet_Practical_Guide_published.pdf. [86]

WP7 core writing group (2020), *D7.2 Guide for the implementation of JA CHRODIS Recommendations and Criteria (QCR) to improve the quality of care for people with chronic diseases. WP7 Fostering quality of care for people with chronic diseases - Task 7.4 Guide for the implementation of Q*. [108]

York Health Economics Consortium (2016), *Cost-Benefit Analysis*, https://yhec.co.uk/glossary/cost-benefit-analysis/. [149]

York Health Economics Consortium (2016), "Cost-effectiveness analysis", https://yhec.co.uk/glossary/cost-effectiveness-analysis/#:~:text=Cost-effectiveness analysis evaluates the,treatments relative to their cost.&text=For example if an intervention,considered to be cost-effective. [150]

York Health Economics Consortium (2016), *Cost-utility analysis*, https://yhec.co.uk/glossary/cost-utility-analysis/. [148]

Yost, J. et al. (2014), "Tools to support evidence-informed public health decision making", *BMC Public Health*, Vol. 14/1, p. 728, http://dx.doi.org/10.1186/1471-2458-14-728. [65]

Youngkong, S. et al. (2012), "Multicriteria Decision Analysis for Including Health Interventions in the Universal Health Coverage Benefit Package in Thailand", *Value in Health*, Vol. 15/6, pp. 961-970, http://dx.doi.org/10.1016/j.jval.2012.06.006. [169]

Yuan, C. et al. (2010), *Blueprint for the Dissemination of Evidence-Based Practices in Health Care - Issue Brief*, The Commonwealth Fund, New York City, https://www.commonwealthfund.org/sites/default/files/documents/___media_files_publications_issue_brief_2010_may_1399_bradley_blueprint_dissemination_evidencebased_practices_ib.pdf (accessed on 21 August 2020). [129]

Annex A. MCDA methodology

This Annex outlines the MCDA frameworks used to identify the set of draft criteria and indicators for public health interventions. Frameworks were identified through a narrative literature review and included:

- Model for Assessment of Telemedicine Applications – telemedicine
- EUnetHTA model – health technology assessments
- RE-AIM model – public and population health
- CDC Conceptual Framework for planning and improving evidence-based practices – public health
- EVIDEM (Evidence and Value: Impact on Decision-Making) – general health
- JA-CHRODIS (Joint Action on Chronic Conditions) criteria to assess good practice – chronic conditions
- The European Innovation Partnership on Active and Health Ageing – European scaling-up strategy – integrated care
- SCIROCCO (Scaling Integrated Care in Context) Maturity Model – integrated care
- EU Best Practice Tool for Public Health
- Canadian Best Practices Portal for Health Promotion and Chronic Disease Prevention
- WHO NCD Research Agenda – NCDs
- European Physical Activity on Prescription (EUPAP) Feasibility Study – physical inactivity
- JANPA self-assessment tool of good practices – childhood obesity prevention programs in kindergartens and schools
- Development of transferability guidance for integrated care models with special focus on Central and Eastern European countries.

A review of applied MCDA frameworks was also undertaken including assessments of: public health interventions in England (Marsh et al., 2013[44]).; primary care in rural/remote areas in Australia (Reeve, Humphreys and Wakerman, 2015[166]); CVD prevention and control policies in Mediterranean countries (Ghandour et al., 2014[167]); tobacco control measures in the United Kingdom (Reddy et al., 2016[168]); and interventions to include in Thailand's national benefits package (Youngkong et al., 2012[169]).Finally, chosen criteria were cross-checked against those identified in a systematic literature review for selecting best practices in public health.

Delegate feedback on best practice criteria

Draft criteria for OECD's Best Practice Identification Framework were presented to delegates to the OECD in October 2019. Results from the vote are summarised in Figure A A.1. The OECD Framework was amended following feedback from delegates, which included outcomes from the vote as well as verbal feedback.

When reviewing results please note:

- "Reach" was re-termed "extent of coverage" in the final OECD Framework

- The criteria "economic sustainability" and "political feasibility" were shifted to the transferability assessment. This was based on delegate feedback who highlighted these criteria were country-specific. For example, if political feasibility were included in best practice framework, performance against this criterion would be of little value to policy makers in implementer context – i.e. knowing the intervention aligned with political priorities within the owner setting is not relevant if these priorities differ from the target setting.
- In line with JA CHRODIS WP 5 ("report on applicability"), the indicators to assess scalability and transferability were considered to be the same, therefore a separate scalability assessment was not developed (JA-CHRODIS, 2017[60]).

Figure A A.1. Importance of criteria for assessing best practice interventions

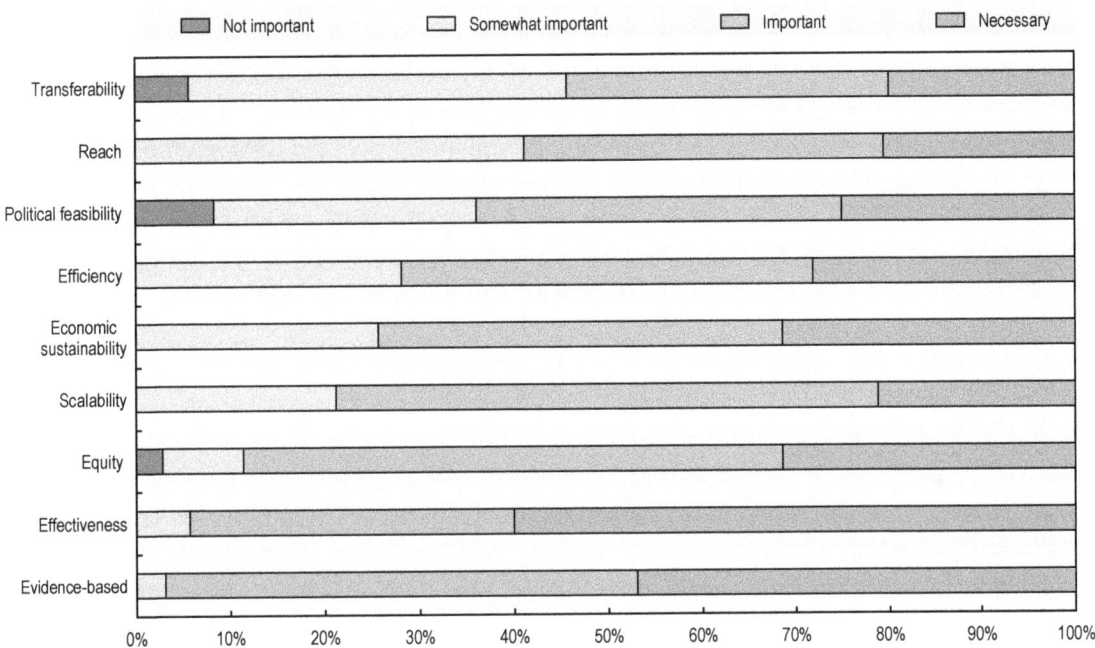

Source: Delegate feedback from Expert Group on the Economics of Public Health (EGEPH) 2019.

Annex B. Outcome indicators

This annex outlines indicators and aligning publically available data sources to assist policy makers identify and evaluate best practice public health interventions (see Table A B.1). To the extent possible, listed indicators are internationally accepted and therefore often routinely collected in a standardised way by countries across the world ("global indicators").

Global indicators are recommended since:

- they allow policy makers to assess and compare the performance of interventions implemented in different countries or contexts
- they reduce administrative burden by relying on routinely collected data sources
- they promote and enhance sharing of information and knowledge, which is particularly important in public health given countries across the world are experiencing similar challenges (for example, heterogeneity in the design of public health intervention evaluations is often cited as a barrier to understanding their overall impact in systematic reviews and meta-analyses).

Indicators can be broken into several categories (e.g. output and outcomes), however, this section focuses on outcome indicators, both intermediate and final, given they are of most interest to policy makers.

In reviewing the list of indicators, it is important to remember:

- the list of indicators is not exhaustive, rather, the list is designed as a 'starting point' for policy makers who are encouraged to review other global indicators using provided links to international databases (see Box A B.1).
- collection of indicators not specified in the list provided or within international databases are encouraged if they are deemed most appropriate within the local context (e.g. lack of required resources, data collection restrictions, specific needs of population groups).

Box A B.1. Publically available databases and resources

This box summarises key publically available sources collecting data on leading global indicators. It is important to note that the recommended databases (and resources) are provided by international organisations and therefore focus on national level statistics. Statistics at the local, municipality or state level, for example, are typically available from a country's national statistical agency, many of which have developed online, interactive statistical dashboards. Countries may also have an organisation dedicated to collecting and/or reporting national and sub-national health statistics.

OECD Health Statistics: OECD Health Statistics provides national-level statistics for OECD and several non-OECD countries covering topics such as health expenditure and financing; health status; health care resources; health care utilisation; and non-medical determinants of health. http://www.oecd.org/els/health-systems/health-data.htm.

Pre-prepared statistics comparing countries across various health dimensions can be found in the following OECD publications: *Health at a Glance: Europe 2018* & *Health at a Glance 2019* (OECD/European Union, 2018[83]; OECD, 2019[84]).

OECD Statistics: in addition to health, OECD provide data for a range of other topics such as education, the economy and productivity. https://stats.oecd.org/.

WHO Global Health Observatory: the WHO publishes data on a wide-range of health indicators for countries across the world. https://www.who.int/data/gho/data/indicators.

World Bank Data (World Development Indicators): the World Bank and has developed a DataBank providing information on a wide range of topics such as health, education, inequality and the economy. https://data.worldbank.org/indicator.

Eurostat: Eurostat's database, Eurobase, provides statistics on a range of topics for European countries. Topics include health, economic and finance, and population and social conditions. https://ec.europa.eu/eurostat/data/database.

European Core Health Indicators (ECHI): ECHI tool includes statistics for Member States covering demography and socio-economic situation, heath status, determinants of health, health services, and health interventions. https://ec.europa.eu/health/indicators/echi/list_en.

European Health Information Gateway (WHO Regional Office for Europe): the European Health Information Gateway combines data for a wide range of health issues such as health literacy, mental health, obesity, pollution, and AMR. It also includes in-depth country profiles for each Member States. https://gateway.euro.who.int/en/.

European Observatory for Health Systems and Policies: the Observatory is a partnership between the WHO, various European Governments, international organisations and academia. It promotes evidence-based decision-making through comprehensive and rigorous analysis of health systems and policies across Europe. The Observatory publish a range of material on country health systems reviews and country health profiles. It also includes an interactive tool allowing users to compare health care systems across different countries (see: https://www.hspm.org/searchandcompare.aspx).

Institute for Health Metrics and Evaluation (IHME): IHME is an independent research centre providing comparable data across a range of health indicators and countries. Data from IHME is publically available and includes information on the global burden of disease by country. http://www.healthdata.org/.

Other useful links

National statistical agencies: a list of national statistical agencies and contact details for European Member States, EFTA countries, candidate countries, potential EU countries and other: https://ec.europa.eu/eurostat/web/links.

The Commonwealth Fund is a privately run foundation designed to promote better performing health care systems. The Fund provides free-to-access international profiles of health care systems. https://www.commonwealthfund.org/publications/fund-reports/2017/may/international-profiles-health-care-systems.

Table A B.1. Global indicators and aligning data sources

Indicator	Category	Dataset	Source within dataset
QALYS gained (see Box A B.2 below)	Universal heath outcome	Participant surveys	n/a
DALYs averted (see Box A B.2 below)	Universal heath outcome	Participant surveys	n/a
Life expectancy	Universal heath outcome	OECD Health Statistics	Health status: life expectancy
Healthy life expectancy	Universal heath outcome	OECD Health Statistics	Health status: healthy life expectancy
Perceived heath status	Universal heath outcome	OECD Health Statistics	Health status: perceived health status
Avoidable mortality	Universal heath outcome	OECD Health Statistics	Health status: avoidable mortality
Change in body mass index (BMI) (= weight / height[2])	Risk factor (obesity)	Objective measurements[1] Self-reported surveys	n/a
% of the adult population who are obese (BMI ≥30)	Risk factor (obesity)	OECD Health Statistics	Non-medical determinants of heath: body weight
% of the adult population who are overweight (25 ≥ BMI < 30)	Risk factor (obesity)	OECD Health Statistics	Non-medical determinants of heath: body weight
% of the adult population who are overweight or obese (BMI ≥25)	Risk factor (obesity)	OECD Health Statistics	Non-medical determinants of heath: body weight
% of school-aged children and adolescents (5-18 years) with a BMI +1 standard deviation from reference median (overweight)	Risk factor (obesity)	WHO Global Health Observatory	Overweight and obesity
% of school-aged children and adolescents (5-18 years) with a BMI +2 standard deviations from reference median (obese)	Risk factor (obesity)	WHO Global Health Observatory	Overweight and obesity
% population who are daily smokers	Risk factor (tobacco consumption)	OECD Health Statistics	Non-medical determinants of heath: tobacco consumption
% population who are occasional smokers	Risk factor (tobacco consumption)	OECD Health Statistics	Non-medical determinants of heath: tobacco consumption
% population who are occasional or daily smokers	Risk factor (tobacco consumption)	OECD Health Statistics	Non-medical determinants of heath: tobacco consumption
Cigarettes smoked per day	Risk factor (tobacco consumption)	OECD Health Statistics	Non-medical determinants of heath: tobacco consumption
Grammes of tobacco per capita	Risk factor (tobacco consumption)	OECD Health Statistics	Non-medical determinants of heath: tobacco consumption
Litres of alcohol consumed per person per year	Risk factor (harmful alcohol consumption)	OECD Health Statistics	Non-medical determinants of heath: alcohol consumption

Indicator	Category	Dataset	Source within dataset
Frequency of alcohol consumption (every day, every week, every month, less than once a month, never or not in the last 12 months)	Risk factor (harmful alcohol consumption)	Eurostat	Indicator code: hlth_ehis_de10
Frequency of heavy episodic drinking (60g of pure alcohol of more in on sitting) (every day, every week, every month, less than once a month, never or not in the last 12 months)	Risk factor (harmful alcohol consumption)	WHO Global Health Observatory	Global Information System on Alcohol and Health
% population who engage in performance enhancing physical activity at least once a week (aerobic and/or muscle strengthening)	Risk factor (physical inactivity)	Eurostat	Indicator code: Physical activity (hth_pha)
% adults (18+) reporting doing at least 150min of moderate-intensity physical activity in a week OR 75min of vigorous-intensity (or a combination of the two)	Risk factor (physical inactivity)	WHO Global Health Observatory	Noncommunicable diseases
% children and adolescents (5-17 years) reported doing at least 60min or moderate to vigorous intensity physical activity daily	Risk factor (physical inactivity)	WHO Global Health Observatory	Noncommunicable diseases
% of the population consuming fruits at least once per day	Risk factor (unhealthy diet)	OECD Health Statistics	Non-medical determinants of health: food supply and consumption
% of the population consuming vegetables at least once per day	Risk factor (unhealthy diet)	OECD Health Statistics	Non-medical determinants of health: food supply and consumption
% of people who consume recommended amount of fruits and vegetables per day (e.g. five portions)	Risk factor (unhealthy diet)	National health surveys	n/a (recommended by WHO (2018[170]))
% of population whose free sugar intake is less than 10% of total calorie intake	Risk factor (unhealthy diet)	National health surveys	n/a (recommended by WHO (2018[170]))
% of the population who consume less than 5grams of salt per day	Risk factor (unhealthy diet)	National health surveys	n/a (recommended by WHO (2018[170]))
Relative reduction in raised blood pressure	Risk factor (unhealthy diet)	National health surveys	n/a (recommended by WHO (2018[170]))
% of the population whose saturated fatty acid intake is less than 10% of total calorie intake (less than 1% for trans fatty acids)	Risk factor (unhealthy diet)	National health surveys	n/a (recommended by WHO (2018[170]))
Average number of calories consumed per day	Risk factor (unhealthy diet)	European Health Information Gateway	European Health for all Database (Lifestyles)
Number of suicides 30 days after discharge for patients diagnosed with a mental disorder	Mental health	OECD Health Statistics	Health Care Quality Indicators: Mental health care

Indicator	Category	Dataset	Source within dataset
Number of suicides 1 year after discharge for patients diagnosed with a mental disorder	Mental heath	OECD Health Statistics	Health Care Quality Indicators: Mental health care
Inpatient suicide numbers for patients diagnosed with a mental disorder	Mental heath	OECD Health Statistics	Health Care Quality Indicators: Mental health care
Suicide rate per 100 000 people	Mental Health	WHO Global Health Observatory	Mental Health

Note: For brevity reasons, only one dataset has been mentioned per indicator. However, it is likely other datasets also provide the same information.
1. BMI figures may be measured or recorded through self-reported surveys (the former being more accurate).
Source: See box on publically available data sources and resources.

> ### Box A B.2. QALYs and DALYs
>
> **Quality-adjusted life year (QALY)**
>
> QALYs are a generic measure of a person or groups state of health. They are frequently used to evaluate the impact of an intervention in terms of change in life expectancy, taking into account quality of life (i.e. QALY = change in life expectancy x quality of life score). A QALY equal to one represents one additional year of life in perfect health (National Institute for Health and Care Excellence, 2020[12]; Sassi, 2006[19]).
>
> **Disability-adjusted life year (DALY)**
>
> DALYs measure the burden of disease using the following equation: sum of years of life lost (YLL) due to premature mortality and years lost due to disability (YLD) for those living with a specific health condition and the associated consequences: DALY = YLL + YLD where:
>
> - YLL = number of deaths x standard life expectancy adjusted for age
> - YLD = number of cases x disability weight x average duration of the case (or until death) (WHO, 2020[171]).
>
> As outlined in under Step 1a ('Effectiveness' – 'Indicators'), the validity and reliability of QALY measurements are often questioned (e.g. due to the methods in which patient data is collected). DALYs are also subject to criticism, for example, favouring immediate over future health benefits, which is disadvantageous for prevention interventions, and weighting that disfavours children and old people.

Notes

[1] Efficacy is a closely related concept to efficiency with the exception that it refers to outcomes achieved in a controlled setting.

[2] For example, see article from Reddy et al. (2016[168]) who used this approach to measure the performance of various smoking cessation interventions.

[3] Core components pivotal to the success of an intervention can be identified through a process evaluation, which is discussed steps 2 and 3 of the guidebook.

[4] If the intervention is not delivered in a health setting, the same analysis can be undertaken for the relevant profession. For example, the skill-set of teachers delivering an intervention regarding the importance of healthy eating and exercise.

[5] Applying an implementation framework to guide the process is one of the recommendations of the EU Joint Action on Chronic Diseases (CHRODIS-PLUS) report that provides recommendations for transferring and implementing good practice interventions (Stegeman et al., 2020[58]). The report also recognises that implementations science can support development of a framework, by helping analyse the context in a good practice will be implemented and how to effectively engage the people who will be affected by the implementation (ibid.).

[6] These are common groups of stakeholders in population-based prevention policies (see, for example, WHO (2010[106])). In general, however, one principle of stakeholder engagement is that, "all significantly affected and potentially interested parties should be consulted" (see Note 7). Which stakeholders to engage therefore depends on the type of intervention.

[7] See draft OECD Best Practice Principles on Stakeholder Engagement in Regulatory Policy, available at http://www.oecd.org/governance/regulatory-policy/public-consultation-best-practice-principles-on-stakeholder-engagement.htm.

[8] SMART = specific, measurable, achievable, relevant and time-bound.

www.ingramcontent.com/pod-product-compliance
Ingram Content Group UK Ltd.
Pitfield, Milton Keynes, MK11 3LW, UK
UKHW050413240426
12048UKWH00020B/1485